Economic evaluations of
unpaid household work:
Africa, Asia, Latin America
and Oceania

Women, Work and Development, 14

Economic evaluations of unpaid household work: Africa, Asia, Latin America and Oceania

Luisella Goldschmidt-Clermont

Prepared with the financial support of the
United Nations Fund for Population Activities
(UNFPA)

International Labour Office   Geneva

ISBN 92-2-105827-1
ISSN 0253-2042

First published 1987

Printed in the German Democratic Republic   ZIM

100424688T

Economic evaluations of unpaid household work:
Africa, Asia, Latin America and Oceania

PREFACE

This volume builds on earlier work by the author on economic evaluations of unpaid household work based on studies from industrialised countries. When this earlier work (Unpaid work in the household: A review of economic evaluation methods)[1] was published as the first volume in the Women, Work and Development series, discussion began on what should be done next. The relevance and importance of this work for the Third World, especially for poor households and poor women, was apparent. For such people, unpaid household activities are not a matter of boosting household welfare and consumption but represent the margin allowing for survival. In addition, due to the abysmally low labour productivity of domestic activities, women in developing countries must devote long hours to back-bending work each and every day, and there are few, if any, days which do not require these tasks to be performed. This burden, in turn, has a deleterious effect on the health of women and on their availability for labour market activities outside the household. Furthermore, because the value of unpaid household work is excluded from the system of national income accounts, national income estimates are incomplete and misleading both over the economic cycle (as families substitute non-market household activities for labour market activities in recessions) and along with economic development (as market transactions and monetary incomes increase in importance); in any case, the sexual and household division of labour between market and household activities cannot be understood without taking full account of household production.

The present volume reviews evaluations from Third World countries in order to help clarify the situation in poorer and less industrialised settings. Before this work was begun, it was unknown how many studies had been undertaken. To our surprise – and clearly due to the persistence and thoroughness of Luisella Goldschmidt-Clermont – 40 such evaluations were found from Africa, Asia, Latin America and Oceania. This treasure-trove of information is the basis for the present book.

The first half of this monograph discusses the different methodological approaches used in economic evaluations of unpaid household work and is essential reading for persons interested in this field. The discussions bring out the difficulties and advantages inherent in each method. The author clearly indicates, however, that she prefers output-based evaluations to input-based evaluations. I fully agree since, if data on household production are eventually to be integrated into national income account statistics, they must be comparable to the latter data; and that implies measuring what is actually produced in the household rather than inferring it from labour inputs. Furthermore, data on household output can be very useful for development planning, labour market planning and raising the status of women. If estimates of labour productivity in household production (combining estimates of output value with estimates of input time) were available, planners would have to face up to the fact that labour productivity in household activities is extremely low; at the same time, they would also have at their disposal information on which household activities are least productive and therefore where policies aimed at increasing labour productivity in household activities would be relatively most effective.

The second part of this monograph contains a review of 40 studies from developing countries. The emphasis is placed on a critical evaluation of the methodological approaches used in these studies, along with excerpts from study results. These summaries are much more than an annotated bibliography and will undoubtedly become a major reference source for persons interested in this field.

It is worth mentioning that these 40 studies provide irrefutable evidence on the importance and value of unpaid domestic and household work. They indicate that a large percentage of total family labour is expended in these activities and that national income estimates would be increased by somewhere between 25 and 50 per cent if the economic value of unpaid household activities were taken into account. Interestingly, this latter figure is very similar to that observed for industrialised countries, as indicated in the author's previous monograph.

This book demonstrates the economic importance of the invisible contribution made in household activities and the fact that women are responsible for most of this work. Until this is recognised, development and labour market planning will be hampered and women's status will be depressed. Fortunately, the author provides us with hope and with useful suggestions on what to do next.

Richard Anker,
Employment Planning and Population Branch,
Employment and Development Department,
ILO,
November 1986.

---

[1] Geneva, ILO, 1982.

CONTENTS

Acknowledgements

This study was supported by the United Nations Fund for Population Activities (UNFPA), the Fonds national de la recherche scientifique (FNRS, Brussels) and the International Labour Office.

I am grateful to Richard Anker for his early recognition of the relevance of this research to ILO concerns and for his continuing interest and support.

Several colleagues helped me in identifying available evaluations and made useful comments on a draft manuscript. I particularly want to thank Derek Blades, Edouard Dommen and Ralph Turvey for their contributions.

Luisella Goldschmidt-Clermont,
Centre d'économie politique,
Institut de sociologie,
Université libre de Bruxelles.

Note: The spelling in all quotations has been standardised according to the ILO's house style.

PART I

CHAPTER 1

INTRODUCTION

1.1 Terminology

This study deals with domestic and related activities and with their corresponding unpaid work inputs. Terminology in this subject-area is unprecise and the scope of domestic activities not clearly defined. We shall not in this study attempt a formal definition but rather be empirically guided by the studies under review.

"Domestic activities", in most studies, include care of children, of the aged, of the ill and of the handicapped, and "housework", i.e. meal preparation (cooking, serving, cleaning up), cleaning the dwelling and its surroundings, care of clothing (laundering, ironing, mending) and all shopping related to these tasks. These activities have several common characteristics. The household's dwelling and its immediate surroundings are the main locus of production and consumption. Labour is supplied by unpaid household members. The goods and services produced are directly consumed by the household or other members of the community without undergoing any monetary transaction.

By "related domestic activities", we mean other productive activities which, in content, mode of production and destination, are similar to the basic core of domestic activities enumerated above. These related domestic activities vary from one society to another. In industrialised countries, they may include, for instance, transportation services (e.g., driving household members to the place of work, to school or to shopping centres). In rural societies, they may include, for instance, water fetching, firewood collection or gathering of wild food.

Domestic and related activities are part of the broader category of own-account productive activities, sometimes also called subsistence, non-market or non-monetary activities.

1.2 Purposes of the study

Policy-makers, economists and statisticians are increasingly aware of the need to account for non-monetary activities.

Throughout the "Forward-Looking Strategies" adopted in Nairobi in July 1985 at the World Conference to Review and Appraise the Achievements of the United Nations Decade for Women, emphasis was placed on the "unremunerated contributions of women to agriculture, food production, reproduction and household activities". In particular, the Conference recommended that "efforts be made to measure and reflect these contributions in national accounts and economic statistics". (United Nations, 1986, paragraph 120.)

The United Nations System of National Accounts (SNA) is under review. Among many other topics, the United Nations Statistical Office "will examine the possibilities and obstacles of further expanding the coverage of subsistence activities beyond the present SNA limits ... The study should build further on present research efforts". (United Nations, Economic and Social Council, 1984, pp. 17-18.)

Economic growth and economic recession modify the nature and extent of non-monetary activities and induce changes in the relative share of goods and services produced for the market and for own-consumption. They also bring about changes in the distribution of labour between the market sector and the non-market sector. In order to monitor these changes, further research is needed for solving the problems connected with the economic evaluation of non-market activities, and in particular of domestic activities.

The present study is a contribution to such research. Economic evaluations of domestic and related activities in Africa, Asia, Latin America and Oceania are reviewed along the lines adopted in earlier studies of evaluations performed mostly in Europe and North America (Goldschmidt-Clermont, 1982 and 1983b). In extending the review to evaluations performed in countries often presenting a lesser degree of market penetration, i.e. of monetisation, two purposes are pursued. The main purpose is methodological: to determine if different evaluation methods were used and if the experience thus gained suggests new ways of tackling evaluation. The second purpose is to have some indication of the orders of magnitude of labour and production at stake in domestic activities versus market-oriented activities.

The evaluations reviewed in the two above-mentioned earlier publications, evaluations scattered over a relatively long period of time (1920-82), were all performed in countries presently classified as industrialised: they did not, however, cover a homogeneous set of economic and social circumstances. Nor do the evaluations reviewed in the present study. It therefore appears preferable to consider each country as having a unique set of characteristics, rather than to think in terms of categories of countries (industrialised, developing or whatever classifications are used for other purposes).

1.3 Economic, social and personal aspects of domestic activities

Domestic and related activities generate an income in kind which plays an unquestionable role in satisfying human needs all over the world. How important is this role? What are the relative contributions of market-oriented activities, of own-account productive activities and, among these, of domestic activities to the satisfaction of these needs?

A single simple answer cannot be given to these questions because of the complexity of domestic activities and of the roles they fulfil. Domestic activities are geared partly to complying with personal needs and social roles, and partly to satisfying economic needs, i.e. producing goods and services which are consumed without going through the market. In the personal and social roles, domestic activities might be considered irreplaceable: performance is tied to personal and social relations and cannot be delegated to an outsider. In the economic role, goods and services produced in the household might, in principle, be substituted by equivalent market products.

In many household work activities, the economic and non-economic roles are intertwined. For example, in some societies, it is the children's duty to care for their aged parents. Social institutions may take over the economic part of this care, but they cannot take over the social function which is tied to the family bond, and which might be perceived as an important loss when care of the aged is transferred to them.

Because of this intertwining of roles, questions arise. Can the economic value of domestic activities be measured? Can they be compared to market activities? As it is not possible to grasp simultaneously, in one measure, the economic, social and personal value of domestic activities, economic evaluations are deliberately limited to the economic dimension.

In order to distinguish which part of domestic activities is economic (i.e. should be considered as production) and which is not, a widely accepted criterion is to determine whether the performance of an activity can be delegated to a paid outsider or not. This criterion, often referred to as the "third person criterion", was introduced by Reid (1934, p. 11).

Household production consists of those unpaid activities which are carried on, by and for the members, which activities might be replaced by market goods or paid services, if circumstances such as income, market conditions, and personal inclinations permit the service being delegated to someone outside the household group ... If an activity is of such a character that it might be delegated to a paid worker, then that activity shall be deemed productive.

The third person criterion was restated by Hawrylyshyn (1977, p. 87):

An economic service (or Z activity) is one which may be done by someone other than the person benefiting therefrom. The question can be asked: can one hire labour to achieve the same results? If yes, then the activity is one which produces Z-goods; if not, the activity is a direct utility one [i.e. producing welfare or satisfaction (p. 77)] and cannot be measured in any meaningful way.

To circumscribe the economic evaluation to economic aspects does not imply in any way that the social and personal values of domestic activities are denied. Furthermore, when utilising economic values for economic purposes, the impact of personal and social values on the nature and extent of domestic activities should be remembered. Conversely, the social functioning of the household cannot be fully understood if the economic aspects of household activities are neglected.

1.4 Organisation of the study

Part I of this volume reviews some 40 evaluations grouped according to the methodology used for the evaluation; it discusses the measurement problems encountered and the solutions adopted. Conclusions are presented on the desirability of performing economic evaluations of domestic activities because of the orders of magnitude at stake, on the feasibility of performing such evaluations and the methods which appear preferable to others. Part II presents summaries of the evaluations under review.

CHAPTER 2

METHODOLOGY OF THE STUDY

2.1 Scope of the study

This study deals with domestic and related activities as defined in 1.1.

It considers "economic" all activities which use the scarce resource labour in order to produce goods and services, i.e. it considers "economic" activities which are outside the production boundary adopted in official statistics (see 2.2).

The study reviews evaluations of productive activities which are infrequently evaluated in economic terms, regardless of the purpose (national accounting or other) for which the evaluations were made.

The evaluations under review were performed in Africa, Asia, Latin America and Oceania.

2.2 The production boundary in the United Nations
System of National Accounts

The United Nations System of National Accounts (hereafter SNA) makes recommendations on which non-monetary activities should be included in the accounts, i.e. on the boundary between what should be considered economic and what should not. This boundary also applies to labour force statistics, as "statistics of the economically active population should comprise all persons of either sex who furnish the supply of labour for the production of economic goods and services as defined by the United Nations System of National Accounts ..." (ILO, Thirteenth International Conference of Labour Statisticians, 1982, Resolution I).

According to the SNA, gross output should include the following own-account production items (United Nations, Statistical Office, 1968, paragraphs 5.13 and 6.19-22):
- own-account production of all primary products, that is the characteristic products of agriculture, fishing, forestry and logging, and mining and quarrying;
- the processing of primary commodities by the producers of these items in order to make such goods as butter, cheese, flour, wine, oil, cloth or furniture for their own use;
- the production of other commodities which are consumed in households that also sell part of them on the market;
- imputed rents of owner-occupied dwellings;
- own-account building and construction.

These recommendations exclude, by default, other own-account production items:
- goods and services (meals, washed clothes, care of children and of the ill, etc.) which are the product of domestic activities;
- the processing, for own consumption, of primary commodities by those who do not produce them;
- own-account production of other commodities consumed in households who do not sell any part of them on the market;
- dwelling and other buildings' upkeep and repair.

On theoretical grounds, it may be argued that there is a rationale in the distinction between own-account productive activities which are to be included in official statistics (i.e. which are to be considered "economic") and those which are not. The position of the production boundary was partly determined by historical factors relating to the purposes the accounts were initially to serve (Keynesian management of the economy). The 1968 revision of the SNA introduced several criteria for determining whether particular activities should be included in the accounts: whether they make a "significant contribution to the well-being of any group of the population" (ibid., paragraph 5.13), or "to the well-being of all groups of the population" (ibid., paragraph 6.20), or whether they raise "marked difficulties of measurement" (ibid., paragraph 5.13). An additional criterion is to ensure the international comparability of national accounts aggregates (ibid., paragraphs 5.13c and 6.19). As a result, an activity which is usually performed on a market basis in industrial countries but on a non-market basis in other countries should be included within the production boundary. This is, however, a criterion which is relevant for international comparisons and need not be allowed to influence the production boundary for national accounts statistics designed for domestic use.

In practice, the profile of the SNA production boundary appears rather sinuous. In rural households where fresh food is prepared daily, the dividing line between food processing (an economic activity) and cooking for the family (not an economic activity) is difficult to draw (Anker, 1983b). Furthermore, while cooking for one's own family is not to be considered an economic activity, cooking food for labourers working on one's farm is included on the ground that food is provided as part of the labourers' wages, i.e. of a market transaction (Mehran, 1986). As with any definition, the definition of the production boundary includes elements of arbitrariness. In this particular case, problems arise because of an effort to categorise some forms of work as non-work and some productive activities as non-economic.

In national accounting practice, the SNA recommendations are only moderately followed. In a survey on the coverage of non-monetary activities, Blades found a considerable variety of coverage patterns among the 70 developing countries which replied to the inquiry (Blades, 1975, tables 2 and 3). Virtually all countries fully cover (at least in principle) own-account agricultural production and rental incomes of owner-occupied dwellings. About two-thirds of the countries also cover other types of own-account primary production (fishing, forestry activities consisting mainly of collecting firewood) and house-building. About half the countries cover own-account food processing (grain milling, beer and wine-making, crushing oil-seeds) and handicrafts (clay pots, wooden tools, furniture, baskets, textiles and clothing). Other own-account activities are less often included. In particular, among tertiary activities, only six countries include water collection, three include crop storage, and two include domestic activities.

There are many reasons for the scarce coverage of some of the non-monetary productive activities in national accounts. Difficulties of "measurement" are explicitly mentioned as a potential obstacle by the SNA; they relate to data requirements (quantity data on the volume of production) and to uncertainty as to the appropriate monetary evaluation methods (price estimates). Countries with little experience and limited means for constructing their national statistics tend to develop first the data relative to market transactions. In doing so, they follow the same process as the countries which started constructing their national accounts some 60 years ago. Nor did the latter countries display much progress in accounting for non-monetary transactions: data collection on own-account construction of dwelling or own-account vegetable gardening (not to speak of the excluded domestic activities) has received very little attention in comparison with the enormous effort invested in the measurement of the monetary sector. This is in spite of the economic "significance" of the contribution these activities make to the "well-being" (total consumption) of the population, even in industrialised countries: the available sporadic evaluations point at combined values for these activities (including domestic activities) of the order of 50 per cent of the gross national product (GNP) as it is presently defined (Goldschmidt-Clermont, 1982; Glaude and Montardier, 1982; Neubauer, 1985).

Quantity and price estimates are not the only obstacles to a fuller integration of non-monetary production into the national accounts framework. Fundamental questions are under discussion, relating to the purposes of national accounting, to the range of activities to be covered, and to the organisation of the data so as best to serve the different uses to which these data are put. While waiting for the current procedure of SNA revision to bring some agreement on these general matters, it would be useful, in the field of domestic activities, to intensify research efforts on evaluation methodology and to perform evaluations compatible with national accounting practice.

2.3 Typology of evaluation methods

Numerous different methods have been used for evaluating domestic activities. In order to present these methods, it is necessary to group them into categories. The typology presented in earlier publications (Goldschmidt-Clermont, 1982 and 1983b) is followed also in the present study. It uses two criteria for grouping the evaluations: the units used for the measurement and the angle from which the evaluation is approached (input or output). By combining these criteria, four main categories of evaluation methods can be distinguished: measurements expressed in physical units yield evaluations of the volume of inputs or of the volume of outputs; measurements expressed in monetary units yield evaluations of the imputed value of inputs or of the imputed value of outputs.

Physical units measuring inputs usually relate to labour inputs: number of workers or number of work-hours. Physical units measuring output are as varied as are household productive activities: number of meals served; of infants or of handicapped persons cared for; weight of laundry washed or of food processed for storage; amount of firewood collected or of water carried, and so on. The first and second categories of evaluations thus comprise evaluations dealing respectively with:

- volume of inputs
     input in workers
     input in time (hours of work)
- volume of output
     in various units, according to activity

All evaluations of household non-market production start with the measurement of physical quantities. Some authors do not pursue this further. The physical quantities thus obtained constitute per se evaluations. The volume of work inputs into household production can then be compared, for instance, to the volume of work inputs into the market sector or into some particular branch of the economy. Or, as another example, the volume of household product in a particular activity (e.g. laundering) can be compared to the output of commercial laundering.

For some purposes, physical units are not convenient to handle: units corresponding to one activity cannot be added to units corresponding to other activities. When the problem of aggregation arises as, for instance, in national accounting, it is solved by resorting to the measurement of values expressed in monetary units.

Values for goods and services produced in the market are determined by market transactions: the socially accepted value is the price at which the transaction is performed. Values for household production are undetermined because there is no price: the labour is unpaid and the product is not sold. In order to express the value of household production in monetary units, it is therefore necessary to borrow values from the market. When measuring inputs, the monetary values borrowed from the market and imputed to unpaid household work usually consist of wages paid for work similar to household work. When measuring outputs, the monetary values borrowed from the market and imputed to household product consist of the prices paid for market goods or services similar to those produced in the household. The third and fourth categories of evaluations thus comprise evaluations dealing respectively with:

- <u>value of inputs</u>
  wages
  returns to labour in other activities
  etc.
- <u>value of output</u>
  price of equivalent market product

The monetary evaluations thus obtained can be compared to macro-economic quantities such as, for instance, GNP or to household income.

In this study, the evaluations under review are grouped according to the framework just described. Table 2.1 summarises the evaluation methods used in the different studies; it is offered as a rough guide to the detailed discussions of Chapters 3 to 5.

2.4 A general comment

A word of caution is required about evaluation results.

Regardless of the evaluation method used, the studies reviewed in this volume differ in many respects:
- by the regions, countries, urban and/or rural settings under study;
- by the population covered by the study (all household members, or only those above and/or below a given age, or only women, or only women with full-time responsibility for domestic activities);
- by the productive activities covered by the study, and their grouping into categories which, from one study to another, are more or less comprehensive or detailed, more or less inclusive (e.g., physical care of children included or not) or more or less overlapping;
- by the data collection methodology (size of sample, representative or not of the total population or of some categories of population, anthropological in-depth observation or social survey approach).

In addition, there are differences in evaluation methodology; they are discussed in the subsequent chapters.

The comparison of evaluation results is seriously hindered by these differences. Also, reservations are often expressed by the authors themselves about their results. Rather than attempting comparisons and extrapolations, it appears preferable to consider each study as unique and to accept its results for what they can contribute, with their geographical, social and cultural limits.

In this manner, the studies under review constitute a very rich source of information on the activity deployed by men and women, the world over, in order to complement their monetary income with non-monetary income towards the satisfaction of their needs. The summaries in Part II of this volume only partly reflect the richness of this information.

Table 2.1: Typology of evaluation methods

Inputs, volume
    volume of labour inputs, in time
    volume of labour inputs, in workers

Inputs, value
    wage, substitute household worker

    wage, equivalent market function
    wage, equivalent market qualifications (a)

    wage forgone or opportunity cost of time

    wage, average for all workers
    wage, average for female workers

    wage, minimum

    returns in other activities (b)

    value of non-cash benefits

    bride price (b)

    labour costs in market enterprises (a)

Output, volume
    volume of output by activity

Output, value
    gross output value, derived from consumer expenditures on
                        material inputs
    value added,   derived from consumer expenditures on
                        material inputs
    gross output value, at price of equivalent market product
    value added,   at price of equivalent market product

Note: Each method found in the present study and in Goldschmidt-Clermont, 1982 and 1983b unless otherwise indicated: (a) method found only among the evaluations reviewed in Goldschmidt-Clermont, 1982 and 1983b; (b) method found only among the evaluations reviewed in the present study.

CHAPTER 3

INPUT-RELATED EVALUATIONS OF HOUSEHOLD
PRODUCTION: VOLUME OF INPUTS

This chapter reviews evaluations which take as a starting-point inputs into household non-market production and which are expressed in physical units, i.e. evaluations measuring the volume of inputs. All evaluations of the volume of inputs reviewed in the present study deal with labour inputs; none deals with other inputs. The volume of labour inputs is measured either in number of workers or in time.

3.1 Volume of labour inputs, in workers

The number of workers involved in domestic activities was used for evaluation purposes in:
Latin America
      Mexico, 1970 (Pedrero Nieto, 1983)
      Pedrero Nieto estimates the number of persons having responsibility for domestic activities in Mexico, by utilising the 1970 census data on persons, mostly women, registered as "not in the labour force". She refines these data by accounting for age and matrimonial status and by comparing the data with census data on number of households, of dwellings, and of families. She reaches an estimate of approximately 9.5 million persons dedicating themselves essentially to the "daily reproduction of the labour force". Total population is estimated at 52 million persons (United Nations, Department of International Economic and Social Affairs, Population Division, 1982). Thus approximately one person out of five, children included, would be required for domestic activities. This estimate does not include persons who are in the labour force and who, in addition, are responsible for domestic activities, nor does it include persons participating in domestic activities without being responsible for them. The contributions of these two categories of people to unpaid household work are substantial, as shown by evaluations of time inputs reviewed in the next section.

3.2 Volume of labour inputs, in time

The number of hours devoted to household production was used for economic evaluation purposes in:

Africa
        Botswana, 1974-75 (Mueller, 1984)
        Cameroon, 1964-74 (Henn, 1978)
        Lesotho, 1976 (Feachem et al., 1978)
Asia
        Bangladesh, 1976-77 (Cain, 1977)
        Indonesia, 1975-76 (Hart, 1980)
        Indonesia and Nepal, 1972-73 (Nag, White and Peet, 1978)
        Nepal, 1972-73 (Nag, White and Peet, 1978)
        Nepal, 1980 (Acharya and Bennett, 1981 and 1983)
        Philippines, 1975-76 (Navera, 1978)
        Philippines, 1975-77 (Evenson, Popkin and King-Quizon, 1980)
        Philippines, 1975-77 (King and Evenson, 1983)
        Thailand, 1980-82 (Evers and Korff, 1982)
Latin America
        Argentina, 1983 (Kritz et al., 1984)
        Bolivia, 1983 (Tellería Geiger, 1983)
        Chile, 1981 (Pardo, 1983; Pardo and Cruz, 1983)
        Chile, 1983 (Martínez Espinoza, 1983)
        Peru, 1983 (Tueros, Hoyle and Kritz, 1984)
        Uruguay, 1983 (Campiótti, 1983)
        Venezuela, 1982 (Valecillos et al., 1983)

Results

    A few results are presented here as illustrations of what is
achieved with these evaluations. They are selected among
evaluations derived from relatively large sample surveys or from
anthropological studies which collected data from a minimum of
100 households and which controlled for seasonal variations. It
should be stressed that results obtained in the context of one
study can by no means be extrapolated to other contexts.
    In southern Cameroon, Henn estimates that, in 1974, the
principal male and female adults in peasant families spend, on
average, 6 hours per day at work.
The women contribute 7.3 hours of work per day; the men 5 hours.
Of total labour time:
        32   per cent is for cash-earning activities;
        44   per cent is for subsistence agriculture;
        24   per cent is for domestic activities.
Wives spend daily 2.7 hours on domestic activities; husbands 0.2
hours.
    In six villages of Nepal, Acharya and Bennett estimate that,
in 1980, the population aged 15 and over spends, on average, 9.3
hours per day at work.
The women contribute 10.8 hours of work per day; the men 7.5
hours.
Of total labour time:
        55   per cent is for "conventional economic" activities
              (animal husbandry, agriculture, manufacturing, wage
              earning, trade);

17   per cent is for "expanded economic" activities
      (hunting and gathering, fuel and water collection,
      dwelling construction, and food processing);
27   per cent is for domestic activities.
Women spend 4 hours daily on domestic activities; men 0.8 hours.

In a village of Nepal, Nag et al. estimate that, in 1972-73,
among the population aged 15 and over, females, depending on age,
spend 11.3-14.1 hours per day at work; males, depending on age,
spend 9.3-11.2 hours per day at work.
Of females' total labour time, depending on age:
28-48   per cent is for "household maintenance"
         (child care, household food preparation, firewood
         collection, and other work).
Of males' total labour time, depending on age:
15-24   per cent is for "household maintenance".
Females spend 3.2-6.9 hours daily on household maintenance;
males 1.6-2.5 hours.

In a village of Bangladesh, Cain estimates that, in 1976-77,
males and females aged 13 and over, depending on age, spend 9-9.5
hours per day at work; no major differences appear in the
work-hours contributed by women or men.
Of total labour time:
45   per cent approximately is for "housework" defined to
      include, in addition to domestic activities, fuel and
      water collection, and food processing.
Females spend 7-7.8 hours per day on such broadly defined
houswork; males 0.7-1.1 hours.

In the ten largest cities of Venezuela, Valecillos et al.
estimate that, in 1982, adult females and males spend
respectively 7 and 6.5 hours per day at work, Sundays and
holidays included.
Females spend 4.75 hours daily on domestic activities; males 0.5
hour. Assuming that there are as many men as women in the
population, of total labour inputs,
39   per cent are for domestic activities.

In Buenos Aires, Argentina, Kritz estimates that, in 1983,
the combined inputs of all household members amount, on average,
to 12 hours per day on unpaid domestic activities, Sundays and
holidays included.
Housewives put in 69 hours per week on domestic activities, i.e.
almost 10 hours per day; employed housewives spend on average 56
hours per week on domestic activities, non-employed housewives 73
hours.
As a point of comparison, the study indicates that, according to
the definitions used for official statistics the normal working
week for paid workers oscillates between 35 and 45 hours,
although more than 1.3 million workers in Gran Buenos Aires have
working weeks of 45 or more hours. Only 12 per cent of
housewives devote less than 40 hours per week to domestic tasks.

Tomoda (1985) rearranges anthropological time-allocation
data so as to present labour force activities in categories as
close as possible to official definitions (United Nations, 1968;

ILO, 1982). She creates an additional category for domestic and related activities. On the basis of data derived from two of the studies grossly summarised above (Acharya and Bennett, 1983, in Nepal; Cain, 1980, in Bangladesh), her study shows the impact of socio-economic and cultural characteristics on time-use.

Several studies point at inter-class differences in the absolute and proportionate amount of time spent by women on housework. For instance, in a village of Indonesia (Central Java), Hart estimates that, in the richer households, in spite of better equipment, women spend more time in housework because of more frequent and more elaborate meals, of more house cleaning in larger and more furnished dwellings, and so on. She comments: "In general, therefore, ... increases in household capital are complemented by a rise in housework time, and this additional time probably contributes substantially to household welfare" (Hart, 1980, p. 203).

Some evaluations illustrate the impact of household composition, household income, educational level, assistance by paid domestic workers or by other household members, and so on, on total time devoted to domestic activities and on its distribution between the various activities. For instance, case studies (Tueros et al., 1984 in Peru; Campiótti, 1983 in Uruguay) observe the higher proportion of time devoted to food-related activities as a percentage of total time devoted to domestic activities in poorer households. Other studies illustrate differences in time-use in different areas of one country. Kritz et al. comment on "the combined impact of the economic recession which increases women's market and non-market activities and of a conservative division of household roles, resulting in a large increase of women's workload and in a reduction of the time specifically devoted to child care" (1984, p. 44).

Other time-use studies

The time-use studies reported above were established for the purpose of evaluating time inputs into unpaid household work. There are, in addition, numerous other time-use studies. To review them here would go beyond the scope of the present study. The question remains nevertheless of how useful they could be for evaluation purposes. Some answer to this question can be found by analysing Minge-Klevana's (1980) survey of anthropological time-allocation studies in industrialising and post-industrial societies up to 1978. After excluding studies which report time in units other than hours, those which measure only one type of activity, and those which do not provide a description of the methods used, she estimates that 29 time-allocation studies are left of which seven deal with households in industrialising societies. Minge-Klevana reports labour time in hours per day, for men and women separately, and for activities "inside the house" (domestic activities) and "outside the house" (including activities directly pertaining to food production).

From Minge-Klevana's data (table 1, p. 281), we calculated the proportion of domestic activities time to total labour time. When applying the same criteria as earlier in this chapter (significant number of households and control of seasonal variations), only two of the seven studies are left. (Only rarely do anthropological observation studies deal with a sufficient number of cases for meeting the requirements of economic evaluations; their contribution, on the other hand, is valuable for the interpretation of larger studies' results.)

One of these two studies deals with a village in Nepal and was already discussed above (Nag, White and Peet, 1978). The second study deals with a village in Mexico (Erasmus, 1955). For men's and women's time combined, domestic activities absorb 53 per cent of total labour time. Women spend 7 hours daily at domestic activities; men 2.7 hours.

Carr, reviewing a number of time-use studies in sub-Saharan Africa, estimates that -

During the rainy season, ... the busiest agricultural season, women spend 9-10 hours a day in the fields. When all other tasks are added to this, it is not surprising to find that rural women work as many as 15 hours a day ... The women's workload during off-peak seasons is only slightly less demanding. Estimates show that when the number of hours spent in the fields is lower, the number of hours spent on other activities such as collecting water and firewood, processing and preparing food and caring for children increases. (Carr, 1985, p. 117.)

Other time-use data were collected not per se but as a basis for establishing monetary evaluations of labour inputs. They are presented in Chapter 4 with the corresponding evaluations.

3.3 Methodological comments

Data collection. These evaluations differ in many respects. In addition to the general differences already mentioned in 2.4 (areas, populations and activities under study), they also present differences specific to time-use studies:

- data collected by direct observation (continuously or at time intervals) or through interviews during which the respondent is asked to recall, for him/herself and sometimes for other household members, the use of time during the preceding day, or days, or week; between fixed hour limits or over the 24 hours of the day;
- days for recall chosen or not so as to represent all days of the week and/or different seasonal patterns of activity;
- all activities recorded, or only activities defined at the start as "productive";

- time devoted to simultaneous activities double-counted or only time devoted to "primary" (i.e. the most important) activities recorded.

Concerted efforts aiming at ensuring comparability between studies performed in different countries are exceptional. The Multinational Comparative Time-Budget Research Project (Szalai, 1972) is perhaps the most famous of these efforts.

The Latin American studies presented at a seminar organised in Lima in April 1984 at the initiative of the ILO Regional Office also present certain common characteristics (ILO, Regional Office for Latin America and the Caribbean, 1984, which includes excerpts of Campiótti, 1983; Kritz et al., 1984; Martínez Espinoza, 1983; Tellería Geiger, 1983; Tueros et al., 1984; Valecillos et al., 1983. Excerpts of Pedrero Nieto, 1983, discussed under 3.1 above, are also included.) Almost all the Lima seminar studies refer to the year 1983 and include all days of the week and all adult members of households living in large urban centres. Most of these studies collect time-use data through structured interviews with housewives. They all include housework, care of children, and health care of adults.

In spite of the effort towards co-ordination, there are however, differences even between the Lima seminar studies. Some are broader in scope than others: the Bolivian study includes time inputs of domestic servants, while the Uruguayan one includes time inputs by non-household members giving unpaid assistance with household activities. The Peruvian study includes care of garden and plants, while the Chilean one further includes repair of dwelling, appliances and vehicles, and care of animals. However, the major differences between these studies relate to sample characteristics: they range from case studies including from eight to 48 households to representative sample surveys including 400 to 1,000 households.

From the methodological point of view, the differences in coverage between the Lima seminar studies are very valuable: they point at aspects which were usually omitted from earlier studies and which should be considered for inclusion. Coverage of these aspects is necessary for obtaining a comprehensive picture of time-use and for understanding the distribution of work inputs by different household members. For instance, unpaid work inputs by non-household members or paid work inputs by domestic servants are usually not included in household production studies. At first glance, they appear to be outside the scope of the studies. However, as they are complementary to unpaid work inputs by household members, when not covered they turn out to be the missing link for interpreting differences in time inputs between households of otherwise similar characteristics (number of children, monetary income, labour force participation, etc.).

Number of workers. Official statistics (census and/or labour force surveys) usually provide the basic data from which the number of workers in unpaid household work is estimated. A common procedure for determining the number of women devoting all of their time to domestic activities is to assume that it is equal to the number of women who are above a certain age and are not in the labour force. However, there are difficulties with this approach. Because of problems relating to data collection and to categorisation of women's activities (Anker, 1983a and b), women's participation in the labour force is underestimated, i.e. the number of women engaged exclusively in domestic activities is overestimated. On the other hand, domestic activities performed by women in the labour force and by other household members (adults or children) are most often neglected. On account of this, the total number of workers involved in domestic activities is underestimated. Whether these overestimates and underestimates offset each other varies from one society to another. Pedrero Nieto in her Mexican evaluation avoids the overestimation pitfalls.

Number of work-hours. One feature of the evaluations reviewed in this section is that work inputs into domestic activities and into market-oriented activities are taken from the same data base, be it a social survey or an anthropological study. This was not the case in earlier studies which relied on labour statistics for time inputs into labour force activities and on special surveys for domestic activities (Goldschmidt-Clermont, 1982, Chapter 3). The use of such different data sources, each with their own methodological and empirical problems, sets serious limits on the precision of the comparison.

Recall vs. observation. An interesting illustration of what differences in data collection methods may amount to is given by the 1975-77 Laguna study in the Philippines. It offers two sets of data: one is obtained from recall interviews in a representative sample survey of 576 households, while the other is obtained by observation in an intensive survey of a subset of 99 households (Evenson, Popkin and King-Quizon, 1980; King and Evenson, 1983).

According to "observation" data:
- of total market time,
  fathers contribute   46 per cent,
  mothers contribute   17 per cent,
  children contribute   37 per cent;
- of home production time,
  fathers contribute   6 per cent,
  mothers contribute   34 per cent,
  children contribute   60 per cent.

According to "recall" data:
- of total market time,
  fathers contribute   63 per cent,
  mothers contribute   22 per cent,
  children contribute   15 per cent;
- of home production time,
  fathers contribute   5 per cent,
  mothers contribute   70 per cent,
  children contribute   25 per cent.

The recall data were collected from the father for market time and from the mother for home production time. Both seem to underestimate the time inputs of others, namely of the children and of their spouse.

The limited aptitude of individuals to recall past activities and to estimate the time they required are among the most intractable difficulties encountered with the recall method.

Simultaneous activities. Several domestic activities are often pursued in parallel. Sweeping a floor, occasionally stirring a cooking pot and keeping its fire supplied with wood, and watching that a crawling child does not hurt himself can all be done simultaneously. In some time-use studies, all these activities are assigned the time in which they occur with the result that days have more than 24 hours. Other studies avoid multiple counting of time by recording only the "main" activity under the time under consideration; however, the drawback here is that some activities do not get recorded at all and that the appreciation of which is the main activity is rather subjective.

Work intensity. Time inputs do not reflect the physical effort required for the performance of a task. As pointed out in the Peruvian study (Tueros, Hoyle and Kritz, 1984), the same amount of time devoted to laundering with a machine or to laundering by hand means something very different in terms of physical work expended. A proposal was made to convert time units into energy units, i.e. into calories expended (Nag, 1972). Nag did not however pursue his proposal. In a later publication with other authors, he states:

> ... a large part of 'household maintenance' represents a 'prior demand' on the household's time which is no less a logico-physical prerequisite of household consumption and/or survival than wage labour, cultivation, and so on; time must be allotted to these activities before the household can consider engaging in activities directly productive of cash or physical produce ... These characteristics make it reasonable to treat any unit of working-time as being equal to any other unit, no matter which household member performs it and no matter what the immediate visible return from it is. Thus the most important measure of the relative contributions of women vs. men or of children vs. adults should perhaps simply be the relative amounts of time spent. (Nag, White and Peet, 1980, pp. 269, 282-3.)

The same position is adopted by Henn (1978, p. 167). Cain (1980), concerned with a similar problem, uses wage rate ratios for correcting distortions in productivity levels of adults and children. (He then estimates output in calories produced, while Nag was proposing to measure input in calories expended.) Cain, however, stresses the limitations of wage rates as measures of productivity. He also stresses the interdependence of housework and of market-oriented work: both are necessary and, when performing housework, children enable other household members to engage in market work.

Distinction between work and leisure. It is a characteristic of industrialisation and urbanisation to separate the spheres of work and leisure, and it is a culturally biased requirement to try and introduce this distinction in the time-use studies of countries with other social and economic backgrounds.

Household survey data vs. anthropological observations. The two approaches provide complementary sets of data (Anker, 1978). In the words of the authors of the representative sample survey in Venezuela, "our study privileges the descriptive perspective, i.e. the formal characterisation of situations as registered by statistical data. This does not deny the usefulness or appropriateness of other focuses or perspectives". (Valecillos et al., 1983, p. 7.)

Categorisation. The need to categorise domestic activities in order to record their time requirements is a serious problem in time-use studies. Different categorisation schemes are used, a situation affecting the comparability of results. For instance, some studies include under "housework": food preparation, cooking, cleaning up, shopping, laundering and ironing, sewing and mending, cleaning and upkeep of dwelling (inclusive of care of garden and house plants, heating, dwelling and appliances repair), and miscellaneous (care of animals, accounting, etc.). Other studies will break down these activities into categories which vary from one study to another. Some studies consider care of children and health care of adults are productive activities; others do not.

Comprehensive labour inputs. Domestic activities are mostly performed by unpaid household members; only few studies include time inputs received as help from relatives not belonging to the household or from other community members. Most of the studies of domestic activities do not record the time inputs of paid helpers. These omissions make it difficult to interpret variations between households and distort the picture of labour distribution and of total time inputs. For instance, the time devoted to cooking by housewives in higher income brackets may be lower than that of housewives in lower income brackets because of the availability of paid help. Some studies record only housewives' time and therefore show the impact of income on their time. However it would also be interesting to know how income effects total cooking time, and for this domestic servants' time should be recorded as well. The same applies to unpaid help received from family members or other community members whose contribution is usually not recorded because they are not household members.

3.4 Conclusions

Domestic activities appear, the world over, to be overwhelmingly performed by women, with relatively minor contributions by men. In the studies under review, women's contribution to domestic activities ranges from two-and-a-half times to 14 times that of men.

Although no quantitative conclusion can be drawn as to total time inputs into domestic activities that would be valid across cultures or across countries, one observation can at least be made. None of the studies reviewed in this section sets time inputs into domestic activities at less than 25 per cent of total labour inputs. In other words, care of children and health care of household members, meal preparation, care of dwelling and of clothing require, as a minimum, 25 per cent of the combined labour of men, women and children.

In rural areas, when related activities such as water and firewood collection and food processing for household consumption are added to domestic activities, the time required can go up to 45 per cent of total labour time.

For Latin America as a whole, domestic activities are estimated to require as much or more time than market-oriented activities (ILO, Regional Office for Latin America and the Caribbean, 1984, p. 3).

From a slightly different perspective, one may say that, because the national accounts do not include domestic activities, GNP figures fall short of the output of 25 to 50 per cent of populations' productive activity.

The interest of these evaluations, from the economic point of view, lies in the indications they give on the consumption of a scarce resource, labour, by domestic activities and by labour force activities. They do not, however, provide indications on the productivity of labour in these activities and therefore on their respective contribution to national income or to household consumption.

CHAPTER 4

INPUT-RELATED EVALUATIONS OF HOUSEHOLD PRODUCTION: VALUE OF INPUTS

This chapter reviews evaluations which take as a starting-point inputs into household production and which are expressed in monetary units, i.e. evaluations measuring the value of inputs. All evaluations of inputs reviewed in the present study deal with labour inputs. The majority of these evaluations impute a monetary value to unpaid household labour on the basis of market wages. A few evaluations are based on returns to labour in other activities, or on non-cash benefits enjoyed by the unpaid household worker, or on the bride price.

4.1 Wage-based evaluations

4.1.1 Wages of substitute household workers

In this method, labour inputs into domestic activities are assigned an imputed value which is the wage a paid worker would earn for performing, in the household, the same activities. The wage can be either that of a polyvalent substitute ("domestic servant") who would perform several domestic and related activities, or that of a specialised substitute (cook, laundress, seamstress, etc.) who would perform only specific tasks.

Wages of substitute household workers were used for evaluating unpaid labour inputs in:

Asia
    Lebanon, 1980 (Lorfing and Khalaf, 1985)
    Nepal, 1980 (Acharya and Bennett, 1981 and 1983)
    Pakistan, 1975-76 (Alauddin, 1980)
    Philippines, 1975-77 (Evenson, Popkin and King-Quizon, 1980)
Latin America
    Chile, 1983 (Martínez Espinoza, 1983)
    Mexico, 1970 (Rendón, 1979)
    Mexico, 1970, 1977-78 (Pedrero Nieto, 1983)
    Venezuela, 1982 (Valecillos et al., 1983)

Results

These eight evaluations differ in many respects. Five of them deal with urban households (Chile, the two in Mexico, Venezuela, and Pakistan) and use wages of substitutes for the evaluation of domestic activities. However, only the two Mexican evaluations are based on straightforward wages (polyvalent substitutes' wages). In Chile, Martínez Espinoza combines wages of polyvalent and of specialised substitutes with wages paid in market enterprises for activities similar to those performed in households (see section 4.1.2); for each category of household activities, he calculates an average wage weighted according to estimates of the skills required and of the time the housewife devotes to various aspects of the activity. In Venezuela, Valecillos et al. combine wages of polyvalent substitutes with average wages of females in service occupations (see section 4.1.4). In Pakistan, Alauddin combines wages of specialised substitutes with an output-related evaluation (see section 5.2.2).

The three other evaluations deal with rural households. The wages of substitutes are not used for the evaluation of domestic activities because of the difficulty of establishing a realistic wage for such services in rural areas where there is ordinarily no market for them. In Lebanon, Lorfing and Khalaf use the wages of agricultural workers in an estimate of women's unpaid field work, an estimate which is incorporated in a global evaluation of women's imputed contribution to household income. In Nepal, Acharya and Bennett use the wages of substitutes for the evaluation of construction (building, repairing, well-digging, etc.). In the Philippines study, no details are given on how the method is used.

The two studies in Mexico and the one in Venezuela apply sufficiently similar evaluation and data collection methods for the results to be comparable. On the basis of substitute household workers' wages:
- Rendón estimates that, in 1970, in Mexico City, household production by housewives amounted to a figure similar to the contribution of the country's agricultural sector to GDP;
- Pedrero Nieto estimates that, in 1978, in Mexico City, housewives produced an income in kind equivalent to 62 per cent of the income earned by women in the labour force;
- Valecillos et al. estimate that, in 1982, in Venezuela, in the nation's urban and rural households, housewives' domestic activities produced an income in kind equivalent to 20 per cent of the national income; and in urban households, all household members' domestic activities produced an income in kind equivalent to 22 per cent of the national income. These evaluations, considered "minimal" by the authors, are very close to the value of the product of the petroleum sector and are much larger than any other single economic sector.

4.1.2 Wages for equivalent market functions

In this method, labour inputs into domestic activities are assigned an imputed value which is the wage paid to workers performing similar activities in market enterprises. The "similarity" of domestic and enterprises' activities is determined on the basis of output and, in some cases, also on the basis of the skills required.

Wages of workers performing, in market enterprises, productive functions similar to those performed by households were used for evaluating unpaid labour inputs into domestic activities in:

Latin America

Chile, 1981 (Pardo, 1983; Pardo and Cruz, 1983)

Chile, 1983 (Martínez Espinoza, 1983)

Venezuela, 1982 (Valecillos et al., 1983).

Dommen (1974) recommends that, as a complement to output-related evaluations in the national accounts of the South Pacific region, wages of workers performing comparable work (i.e. requiring a similar level of skills) be used for activities where the market price cannot be satisfactorily determined (repair services, housebuilding, and other construction).

Results

The Chile 1981 and Venezuela studies apply sufficiently similar data-collection methods for the results to be put side by side, although the selection of market wages leaves much room for potential discrepancies. On the basis of wages paid to workers performing, in market enterprises, functions similar to household productive activities,

- Pardo and Cruz estimate that, in 1981, in Chile's urban and rural households, all household members' domestic activities produced an income in kind equivalent to 30 per cent of the "gross geographical product";

- Valecillos et al. estimate that, in 1982, in Venezuela's urban households, all household members' domestic activities produced an income in kind equivalent to 34 per cent of the national income.

4.1.3 Wage forgone or opportunity cost of time

In this method, labour inputs into domestic activities are assigned an imputed value which is the wage the unpaid household worker would have earned if he/she had worked in the market instead of working in the household. This evaluation method therefore adopts a very different approach from the one adopted in the evaluations reviewed in the preceding sections (4.1.1 and 4.1.2), which were based on the hypothetical substitution of an unpaid worker by a wage worker. The forgone wage method (also called opportunity cost of time method) is based on the hypothetical substitution of activities: labour force activities for domestic activities. The method is derived from econometric research on consumer behaviour and time-allocation (Becker, 1965, Lancaster, 1966, and followers of the "New Home Economics" school of thought). Home activity models are constructed on the assumption that, under specified restrictive circumstances, households allocate time so as to maximise returns. As a result, it is assumed, that if a household member works in the household rather than in the market, it is because returns from unpaid household work are perceived as equal or higher than those from market work. Utility derived from the forgone market wage is therefore assumed to be smaller than or equal to utility derived from unpaid household work, and the forgone market wage, or opportunity cost of time, is assumed to reveal the monetary value the household places on the allocation of its members' work time to household production.

The opportunity cost of time method was used for evaluating unpaid labour inputs into household production in:

Asia

>Malaysia, 1976-77 (Kusnic and Da Vanzo, 1980)

>Philippines, 1975-77 (Evenson, Popkin and King-Quizon, 1980; King, 1978; King and Evenson, 1983; Ybañez-Gonzalo and Evenson, 1978)

Latin America

>Chile, 1981 (Pardo, 1983; Pardo and Cruz, 1983)

>Chile, 1983 (Martínez Espinoza, 1983)

>Mexico, 1970, 1977-78 (Pedrero Nieto, 1983)

>Venezuela, 1982 (Valecillos et al., 1983)

Results

Three of the Latin American studies derive their data from a population census or large sample survey. None of the three uses a "pure" opportunity cost: even for employed housewives, the actual wages they earn in the market are not used. Valecillos et al. use average wages in their occupation for employed housewives, and average wages of all female workers for non-employed housewives. Pedrero Nieto uses average wages of females of the same educational level as the housewives under consideration. Pardo and Cruz account, in addition, for age and labour market experience. In spite of these differences in the determination of the opportunity cost of time, the results of these three studies can be looked at side by side. On the basis of opportunity cost of time:

- Pedrero Nieto estimates that, in 1978, in Mexico City, housewives produced an income in kind equivalent to 193 per cent of the income earned by women in the labour force;

- Pardo and Cruz estimate that, in 1981, in Gran Santiago, housewives produced an income in kind equivalent to 18 per cent of the "gross geographical product";

- Valecillos et al. estimate that, in 1982, in Venezuela:

  - in the nation's urban and rural households, housewives (alone) produced an income in kind equivalent to 37 per cent of the national income;

- in urban households (only), all household members
produced an income in kind equivalent to 41 per cent of
the national income.

In the Malaysian study, the opportunity cost of time method
is used in combination with an output-related evaluation (see
section 5.2.2). Opportunity cost of time is used only when it is
not possible to determine gross output value, that is only for
cottage industry products consumed by the household for which a
physical description was not provided in the survey, for
housework, and for cooking and child care. The wage rates of
employed household members are used for defining the opportunity
cost of time of all household members. On this basis:
- from Kusnic and Da Vanzo's data, we calculate that in
Malaysia's urban and rural households in 1976-77, domestic
activities of all adult members generated an income in kind
approximately equal to 40 per cent of households' monetary
income.

In the Philippines' studies, the wage rates of employed
household members (father, mother and children) are used for
defining the opportunity cost of time of all household members.
On this basis:
- Evenson et al. estimate that, in 1975-76, in the
Philippines, in Laguna rural households, the domestic
activities of father, mother and children generated an
income in kind of approximately equal value to monetary
income.

4.1.4 Average and minimum wages

In this method, labour inputs into domestic activities are
assigned an imputed value equal to average market wages or to
minimum market wages. This approach is very close to the
opportunity cost of time approach just discussed above. Indeed,
the two approaches have sometimes been used in a complementary
way: in evaluations based on opportunity cost of time, average
wages were sometimes used for imputing a value on unpaid
household workers' time whose potential market wage is
undetermined because they have no market employment. In
classifying the evaluations under review in this study, we
adopted the criterion that when average wages are calculated
taking into account educational level, labour force experience or
occupation, the evaluation is discussed under opportunity cost of
time, while all other evaluations using average wages are
discussed in the present section. The average wages selected for
imputation are the average for all workers or for female workers
only, in all or in particular sectors of the economy.

Average wages were used for evaluating unpaid labour
inputs into household production in:
Latin America
Venezuela, 1982 (Valecillos et al., 1983)

Minimum wages were used for evaluating unpaid labour inputs in:
Africa
Botswana, 1974-75 (Botswana, 1976; Dahl, 1979)
Oceania
Kiribati and Tuvalu, 1972-74 (Gilbert Islands, 1979)
Papua New Guinea, 1960-74 (Papua New Guinea, 1974)
Fisk (1975b) recommends that, in conjunction with the output-related evaluations of national accounts, minimum wages be used, in the Pacific region accounts, for the evaluation of labour inputs into house construction and maintenance.

Results

In the Venezuela study, Valecillos et al. combine average wages of females in service occupations with wages of substitute household workers (for results, see section 4.1.1); they also combine average wages of all females with the opportunity cost of time (for results, see section 4.1.3).

In the Botswana and Papua New Guinea national accounts studies, minimum rural wages are used in combination with output-related evaluations, only for estimating labour contributed by household members in own-account construction.

In the Kiribati and Tuvalu accounts the average wages of unskilled rural labour, adjusted by a coefficient to allow for variations in energy and concentration, are used for estimating own-account production of dwelling and other capital repairs, handicrafts, thatching, breadmaking and carrying water; identifiable cash inputs are further deducted.

4.1.5 Methodological comments on all
      wage-based evaluations

Non-market services. Wage-based evaluations share one common perspective: domestic activities are perceived as a production of services, more precisely a production of non-market services. The evaluation method consisting of imputing market wages to unpaid household work is inspired by the treatment of other categories of non-market services in national accounting, such as, for instance, government services which are not sold to the public. "The value of the gross output of the producers of ... government services ... is taken to be equivalent to the costs of producing these services" (United Nations, Statistical Office, 1968, paragraph 6.41). We question the application of this treatment to unpaid domestic services because there are major differences between government services and household services.

Government services are produced with market-regulated wages. They are therefore only partly non-market: only their output is non-market. Household services are entirely non-market: input and output are non-market. Market factors and political factors directly bear on the production of publicly funded services, while the impact of such factors on the production of household services is indirect and probably much less determinant.

Another major difference between public institutions and households is that, in addition to services, households produce goods which ought to be accounted for in the same way as goods produced in manufacturing industries, i.e. according to output. This is not the place to discuss whether there is, in general, a clear-cut difference between goods and services, and whether it justifies a different treatment in national accounting practices. (There is an ongoing, and at present unresolved, debate on this among national accountants.) In the limited field of domestic activities, with which this study is concerned, the distinction between goods and services is not obvious: is meal preparation the production of services (i.e. procuring raw foods, cooking, cleaning up, etc.) or the production of goods (i.e. edible meals)? To consider domestic activities only as a production of services is arbitrary, although the approach may appear convenient to some authors for evaluation purposes. It is interesting to note that, among the evaluations reviewed in this section, some use wage-based evaluations only as a last resort method when it is not possible, because of lack of data, to perform an output-related evaluation.

Volume of labour inputs. In order to impute market wages to unpaid household labour, all wage-based evaluations first need to determine the volume of labour inputs. Wage-based evaluations therefore share the problems discussed in section 3.3: the estimate of the number of workers involved in domestic activities; the measurement of time inputs; the handling of simultaneous activities; work intensity, the distinction between work and leisure (utility derived from the use of time); differences in population covered, in activities covered and their categorisation, etc. The quality of wage-based evaluations strongly depends on the quality of the volume of inputs data on which they rely.

Selection of market wages. Two problems arise in this respect. The first is technical: it is no easy task, particularly in countries where the statistical apparatus is relatively modest, to determine wage rates actually paid and representative for the area or for the population under consideration.

The second problem is methodological: the categories of wages selected for the imputation (wages of substitute household workers, of workers performing similar activities in market enterprises, forgone wages, etc.) greatly affect the outcome of the evaluations.

The impact of wage selection on the outcome of the evaluation is best perceived in the studies which apply different categories of wages to the same data base. It is no surprise to discover that the value of domestic activities increases as the wages used for the imputation are located in a higher position on the wage scale. Minimum wages and domestic servants' wages give the lowest evaluations, rural wages and female wages result in lower evaluations than those based on average wages of all workers, and so on. <u>The differences between the imputed values</u> of domestic activities obtained with different wage bases <u>reflect the wage structure of the labour force</u> in the market sectors of the economy. In countries where industrialisation only reaches limited circles of the labour force, wage differentials between the public and modern sectors, the urban informal sector and the agricultural sector may be large. These differentials stem from complex mechanisms related, among others, to intersectoral productivity differentials, the existence of an abundant supply of unskilled labour coupled with inadequate bargaining power, limited access to formal education and to the corresponding privileged employment opportunities, and negative social values attached to certain kinds of labour. These mechanisms affect the wages used for imputing values to unpaid household work and therefore also the outcome of the evaluations.

A question then arises, which will be discussed in section 4.1.6: Is any category of wages more appropriate for the evaluation of unpaid labour inputs into household production?

<u>Imputation of current labour market wages.</u> For aggregate-level evaluations, the soundness of using wages which are linked to a given labour market is sometimes questioned. The argument goes like this: if, for instance, all unpaid housewives became paid domestic servants, or if all unpaid housewives sought employment and hired substitutes to perform domestic activities in their households, such major shifts of labour demand and supply might cause changes in wage rates and invalidate the corresponding evaluations of unpaid household work. This argument implies that in order to use market wages in an imputation one has to assume a complete and instantaneous transfer of labour from unpaid to paid activity. We consider this an unnecessary assumption. Transfer of labour from unpaid to paid activity (and vice versa) is a continuous and gradual process which constantly causes changes in wage rates. On the curve of these wage rate changes, one may determine, at one point in time and space, the market value of labour inputs without having to be concerned about what this value will be at another point in time.

Besides, this situation is not specific to value imputations. It pertains to all economic measurements: the prices used are the current ones and the fact that they might become different in other circumstances is not taken into consideration.

<u>Comparability of results.</u> The comparability of results obtained with wage-based evaluations is hindered by several factors: first, by differences (recalled above) in the assessment of the volume of labour inputs; secondly, by differences in the wages adopted for the imputation (this factor is a major obstacle to international comparisons when the wage

structures of the countries to be compared are different); and thirdly, by differences in the presentation of results (depending on the studies, the value of domestic activities is expressed as a percentage of national income, household income, income earned by women in the labour force or some other reference value; the variety of reference values reflects the variety of purposes for which the evaluations were made).

4.1.6 Methodological comments on particular wage-based evaluations

Discussion of evaluations based on wages of substitute household workers

In all countries, domestic workers' wages are amongst the lowest wages. Without attempting an exhaustive explanation, a few factors may be pinpointed which contribute to this situation.

Domestic activities require skills which are acquired, at home, by younger members of the household as they watch and assist older members. Training is therefore widely available and the labour supply able to meet domestic activity requirements is abundant; it includes practically all females, i.e. half the population. An abundant labour supply not only reduces the bargaining power of the workers; it also contributes to the social undervaluation of the corresponding skills, in contrast to what happens in economic activities requiring a formal training accessible only to a small fraction of the population. Paid domestic workers are further disadvantaged in their bargaining position because they are isolated and because of the personal relationships tying them to their employer.

In countries with high levels of employment and labour demand by the modern sector, the factors contributing to keep down domestic servants' wages are partly offset by the development of other economic sectors: if domestic servants' wages do not keep up with other wages, domestic servants tend to move to better-paid jobs.

In countries where the development process reaches only limited circles of the labour supply, the supply of domestic servants remains large and their wages low. Domestic servants may be available at such low wages that upkeep (food, a place under the roof, some clothing, care in case of illness, and occasional presents) may be the main item of their cost to the employer. Such situations clearly show that evaluations of domestic activities based on wages of substitute household workers should include wages in kind in addition to monetary wages. In extreme cases, observers sometimes claim that there are no paid domestic workers. Assistance in the performance of domestic tasks is received when necessary from non-market community networks of support: unpaid relatives, neighbours, or other members of the community, joining the household permanently or not and receiving or not informal compensation for their work contribution.

A further factor contributing to the low level of domestic servants' wages is the overall tendency for women's wages to be lower than men's wages, as indeed in most countries domestic service tends to be a female profession.

The appropriateness of domestic servants' wages for evaluating housewives' services is questioned by several authors on the ground that they result in undervaluations of domestic activities. These authors consider that housewives' qualifications and responsibility level are higher than those of domestic servants. And also that some social or personal aspects of domestic activities cannot be captured by purely economic measures: for instance, the value of caste purity in food preparation or the value of maternal care. In relation to this latter concern, it should however be remembered that economic evaluations only claim to capture that part of household productive activity which can be delegated to others (see section 1.3).

To conclude, it may be said that, in spite of all these difficulties real wages (i.e. in kind and in cash) of substitute household workers - when they can be assessed - probably offer the most acceptable wage basis for assessing the value of labour inputs into domestic activities.

However it is a mistake to equate, as is often done, the value of labour inputs with gross output value or with value added in household production (see section 4.1.5, non-market services): household workers' wages are determined by labour market factors which bear no relation to the value of household output. Indications in this direction are given by case studies conducted in an industrial area (Goldschmidt-Clermont, 1983a): returns to labour in non-market household production were found to range from a fraction of housekeepers' wages to as much as four times these wages. The link between household workers' wages and the value of their output is probably even weaker in economies offering limited employment opportunities.

Discussion of evaluations based on wages
for equivalent market functions

Evaluations based on wages paid for equivalent market functions assume that the performance of a certain task (cooking, ironing, etc.) commands a specific wage. This assumption is more valid in some countries than in others.

In industrialised economies, it is not valid because it disregards important differences in the circumstances in which households and market enterprises operate. Households furnish small-scale personalised services, they have low overhead and distribution costs, and their productive activities are determined, in part, by non-economic considerations (social roles, personal tastes, etc.). Market enterprises, on the

32

contrary, almost exclusively operate according to economic considerations: monetary accountability with its rewards for scale economies, investments in labour-saving equipment, and so on. The wages they pay are only partly task-dependent: many other factors, among them labour productivity and collective bargaining, play an important role. In monetary terms, economic productivity probably is higher in market enterprises than in households. Workers performing, in commercial enterprises, activities similar to those performed in the household are in a better bargaining position than domestic servants because they are not isolated and because commercial enterprises operating in higher productivity circumstances (higher capital/labour ratio) can afford to pay higher wages than households. As a result, in industrialised economies, wages in service industries adjust to the overall increase of average wages. (For a discussion of labour productivity in the services and of its relation to non-market household production, see Skolka, 1976a, 1976b and 1985b).

In contrast to what happens in industrialised economies, in countries or areas where modern sector employment opportunities are only available to limited sections of the labour supply, the wage adjustments just described do not occur. Service enterprises usually operate in the informal sector: they use equipment similar to that used in households, labour productivity is close to that of the household, the labour supply is plentiful, and workers' wages remain close to those of domestic servants.

To conclude, the wages of workers performing in market enterprise activities similar to household activities are not a satisfactory basis for the evaluation of unpaid labour inputs into domestic activities. This is so in industrialised countries, mostly because of productivity and wage adjustment considerations. In other countries, it appears preferable, for evaluation purposes, to use domestic servants' wages because they apply to the production circumstances of the household rather than to the circumstances of informal sector enterprises.

Discussion of evaluations based on
opportunity cost of time

The application of traditional demand theory to the determination of the value of time (defined as the marginal rate of substitution between time and money) raises measurement problems. De Serpa (1971; expounded by Turvey, 1972, pp. 32-33) argues that it is not possible to measure the "value of time", but only the "value of saving time".

The use of this value for the economic evaluation of domestic activities raises problems even in the context of Western industrialised societies where the "New Home Economics" theory was elaborated (see discussion of forgone wage or opportunity cost of time in Goldschmidt-Clermont, 1982, pp.

23-26). These problems are more acute in the context of societies with different social values and with a different economic structure (Henn, 1978, pp. 169 and 176; Oppong, 1982, pp. 135-7).

Maximisation of returns. The fundamental assumption on which the theory is constructed is that households allocate time so as to maximise returns. The very concept of returns maximisation is culturally bound: it may be verified in societies, or in particular groups of societies, where values of achievement, competition, personal initiative, social mobility, and so on, are praised. But the concept of maximisation of returns is not exportable, for instance, to societies valuing conformity to tradition, community life and support, and which are not favourable to the achievement of higher personal standards of living than the common standards.

Possibility of substituting market and non-market work. Another fundamental aspect of the theory is that it is based on the marginal value of market time, that is on the value of the last unit of market time which, in equilibrium, is assumed to be of equal value to the last unit of non-market time. This implies that market and non-market work can be substituted the one for the other, in units, until equilibrium is reached. The possibility of substituting market time and non-market time in units is questionable even in economies where employment opportunities are plentiful, because of labour market rigidities and because of rigidities in the performance of domestic activities (lumps of time are required, e.g., for preparing meals needed at specific times every day and not in big batches at moments convenient for the household worker), rigidities which limit the required freedom to "choose" how best to allocate the marginal time units or even any time units at all. And indeed, apart from not being substitutable in units, non-market time is, in part, not substitutable at all. Even in the most industrialised economies where division of labour is high and where the market, in principle, can provide for all human needs, a certain amount of non-market time is necessary for survival: in theory, at least the time required for procuring the household with market goods and services is non-substitutable. In practice, time-use studies show that households utilise much more than this minimum for domestic activities. Non-market time appears largely as complementary to market time and is governed by other criteria than market time.

In economies where employment opportunities are not widely available, the assumption of substituting market and non-market work cannot at all be made. Market work provides a monetary income with which certain desirable goods and services can be purchased that cannot be acquired without money (e.g., industrial goods such as machinery, radios, pharmaceuticals, petrol, electricity, etc.). Non-market work provides goods and services which cannot be purchased because the market does not provide substitutes for them (e.g., care of children, of the ill or of the handicapped, cooked food, in some cases water, etc.). In

34

between these extremes, there are goods and services which households do produce because they do not have the necessary money for purchasing a market substitute while they can mobilise unpaid household labour for producing on own-account and/or because they prefer the goods or services produced in the household. Households with limited monetary resources tend, as much as possible, to forgo expenses and to produce on own-account even if the returns per hour of work are lower than the potential hypothetical market wage. In the latter economies, it appears much more clearly than in the more industrialised economies that non-market work and market work belong to two distinct - although related - labour markets, and that time allocation between the two need not be governed by equal returns at the margin.

Undetermined opportunity cost of time. This method cannot directly determine the opportunity cost of time of unpaid household workers who are not gainfully employed and therefore have no observable market wage. This is for instance the case of women devoting all of their labour to domestic activities. In order to solve this problem, the wages of workers with similar characteristics (sex, age, education, labour market experience, etc.) are applied to the non-employed. This solution is in contradiction with the theory itself, which rests on the hypothesis that when a household allocates the labour of one of its members exclusively to domestic activities, it is precisely because the marginal returns are higher there than in market activities. In the frame of this theory, non-employed household workers should be assigned, at the margin, a higher opportunity cost of time than those employed in the market. But this too would be an unsatisfactory procedure because the employed are not necessarily the least productive in household work, but are more probably those who command a higher wage in the market or even just those who can command any kind of wage at all.

Real household output vs. potential market output. Wage-based evaluations are supposed to yield the value of labour inputs into household activities as a proxy to the value of household output. Opportunity cost of time, however, gives the value of the potential market output for a given amount of time, not the value of household output. This particularity is best illustrated by the observation that a given output carries different values depending on who produced it: for instance, it will carry a higher value if it is produced by a more educated person (commanding therefore a higher market wage) than by a less educated person. The imputed value is not related to the characteristics of the household activity nor to the activity-related skills of the unpaid worker, but rather to his/her qualifications for labour market work.

To conclude, the opportunity cost of time method is based on assumptions which are not generally verified, particularly not in economies where employment opportunities are scarce. It does not provide the value of labour inputs into household production but a lower limit of this value, and this only in the exceptional cases where the above-mentioned assumptions are verified.

Discussion of evaluations based on
average and minimum wages

Evaluations based on average wages or on minimum wages share
one major characteristic with evaluations based on the forgone
wage: they relate to the value of a potential market output, not
to household output. They, however, do not require the
assumptions, maximisation and others, of the opportunity cost of
time method. The assumption here is that the average value of
market work time approximates the value of unpaid work time.

At the macro-economic level, to assume that all work time,
market and non-market, has the same average value may be an
acceptable approximation for determining, at one point in time
and space, the market value of labour inputs into household
production (not the value of household production).

At the household level, wages do not represent the value of
market time; labour-related expenses may be far from negligible
in market work, particularly when market work entails migration.
Labour-related expenses should therefore be deducted from gross
wages in order to have the net value of market time. But then a
paradox is raised: the imputed value of unpaid household work
decreases when expenses related to market work increase. In
fact, it is the value of market time which decreases when its
related expenses increase. The paradox stems from the evaluation
method and becomes apparent in the dynamic situation of changing
labour-related expenses. Quite to the contrary of what
evaluations based on this method may indicate, at the household
level, the higher the market-related expenses, the more it pays
to forgo them by producing on own-account, and therefore the
higher the value of unpaid household work.

To conclude, average wages yield, at the macro-economic
level, the market value of unpaid labour inputs into household
production. They do not yield the value of these inputs at the
household level, nor the value of household production because
they are related to labour market factors and not to household
production circumstances.

4.2 Returns in other activities

In this category, we group studies which, after having
measured the volume of labour inputs into household production,
value it at the returns in other activities for which monetary
values can be readily determined. For instance, labour time in
domestic activities is measured and then valued at the hourly
returns to labour in subsistence agriculture. The returns used
for the imputation are sometimes returns to labour only and
sometimes returns to all production factors.

We also include in this category studies which calculate the
returns in market-oriented activities similar or identical to
domestic activities, although these studies do not actually

proceed with an evaluation of non-monetary domestic activities themselves.

Returns in other activities were used for evaluating domestic activities in:

Africa

    Botswana, 1974-75 (Mueller, 1984)

    Cameroon, 1964-74 (Henn, 1978)

Asia

    India, 1970-71 (Mukherjee, 1983)

    Philippines, 1975-76 (Cabañero, 1978)

    Blades (1975, p. 63), discussing the use of labour inputs for estimating non-monetary output, concludes that time devoted to a particular non-monetary activity can only be valued realistically in terms of other non-monetary activities lending themselves to output-related evaluations. He recommends this because other non-monetary activities are the only alternative type of "employment" available.

Returns in market-oriented activities similar or identical to domestic activities were calculated, but not used for evaluating domestic activities themselves, in:

Africa

    Nigeria, 1976 (Longhurst, 1982)

Asia

    Indonesia, 1972-73 (Nag, White and Peet, 1978)

    Indonesia, 1975-76 (Hart, 1980)

Results

Mueller uses returns to labour and to capital in subsistence agriculture and in cash-earning activities for assigning a value to time in the household production function. She estimates that, in Botswana's rural households in 1974-75, the marginal productivity of male labour comes to approximately 0.18-0.22 Pula per day while the marginal productivity of female labour is slightly lower.

As a point of comparison, Lucas (1981, p. 13) finds average rural wages for persons with 0-4 years of education to be 1.26-1.50 Pula per day for men, and 0.54 Pula per day for women. Mueller comments that, opportunities for wage labour being quite limited, asset-poor households often use family labour for non-monetary activities to a point where the marginal returns from work are very low.

Henn uses average hourly returns to labour in non-monetary and in cash-earning activities, in combination with an output-related evaluation (see section 5.2.2). They are used for imputing a value to domestic services because most of them are not sold in rural or urban markets and it is therefore not possible to establish an output-related evaluation for these services. On the basis of average returns to labour in other activities, from Henn's data we calculate that, in southern Cameroon in 1974, domestic activities performed by the principal male and female adults in peasant families add an income in kind of about 30 per cent of their combined incomes in cash-earning and in non-monetary activities, i.e. 65 per cent of their monetary income.

In order to present these results in a comparable way to Henn's evaluation of time inputs (see section 3.2), one may say that total household income is derived as follows:

35 per cent from cash-earning activities,
42 per cent from subsistence agriculture,
23 per cent from domestic activities.

Mukherjee uses the average annual contribution to net domestic product (NDP) per worker in agriculture. On this basis, it is estimated that, in India in 1970-71, the domestic activities of women aged 14 and over and married produced an income in kind equal to approximately 33 per cent of NDP.

Cabañero calculates the gross output value of home-produced goods which are consumed by the household and are also sold on the market (farm tools, home-sewn clothes, cooked food, laundry, etc.). She finds that returns to labour in household production are, in general, higher than market wages for all income groups.

Longhurst calculates returns to labour hours in the preparation of cooked food for sale by housewives (i.e. under the same technological circumstances as food cooked for own-consumption). He finds that in the Muslem Hausa village under consideration, food cooking yields returns comparable to women's wages for planting crops.

Nag et al. calculate returns per hour of labour in market-oriented activities on the basis of prevailing prices and wages. They find that, in the Javanese rural households under consideration, food processing (a market-oriented activity also performed for own-consumption and similar to the domestic activity "food preparation") yields very low returns to labour compared to returns to labour in agriculture. For instance, the hourly returns in preparation of fried cassava and of fermented soybeans are respectively of 3.5 and 5 Rp, while the returns in rice cultivation are of 12.5 Rp for share-croppers. From the economist's point of view, returns to share-croppers' labour are the most adequate for comparison with returns to labour in food preparation because they only include returns to labour, while owner-cultivators' returns include, in addition, returns to capital. From the household point of view, the owner-cultivator considers his aggregate returns without separating returns to labour from returns to capital.

Hart calculates returns to labour per hour on the basis of wages for wage labour and on the basis of market prices for searching activities (fishing, gathering wild vegetables, snails and fuel); she takes travelling time into account. She finds that, in the Javanese rural households under consideration, searching activities yield lower returns than wage labour; however, in the poorer households, the ratio of returns only fluctuates between 1.5 and 2 in favour of wage labour.

Methodological comments

The imputation to domestic activities of returns to labour in other activities is based on the assumption that all types of labour inputs are equally important for family welfare, an assumption similar to that of Henn and Nag et al. for the treatment of time inputs (see section 3.3, work intensity). The latter authors present it as "an extension of Chayanov's (1966) notion that the peasant family farm receives for the sum total of its labour inputs a 'single labour income' which cannot realistically be decomposed into separate components" (Nag, White, and Peet, 1980, p. 283).

Blades' recommendation to use returns to labour in non-monetary activities only (and not in market-oriented activities) has the advantage that such returns are not directly determined by labour market factors, but rather by production circumstances which are close to those of domestic activities.

Returns to labour in market-oriented household production of goods and services similar or identical to those produced for own-consumption are even preferable, when available, to returns in other non-monetary activities because, in addition to being performed in similar production circumstances, they also generate the same output.

The valuation of domestic activities at returns in other activities constitutes, from the point of view of our typology, a mixed approach. It belongs to the category "input-related evaluations of household production" because it is based on an initial measurement of the volume of inputs. It departs from other evaluation methods in this category, because the imputed value is derived not from labour input values (wages), but from output values (outputs of other activities).

In this approach, the purpose is to estimate the value, not of unpaid labour inputs, but rather of household output. The approach cannot, however, be categorised as output related in our typology, because it is not based on an initial measurement of household output. It is instead assumed that returns in domestic activities are equal to those in other selected (monetary and/or non-monetary) activities and the value of household domestic output is, in fact, derived from the volume of labour inputs.

The evaluation method imputing returns in other activities has the advantage over other input-related evaluation methods of yielding results related to an actual output. Although this output is not the output of domestic activities themselves it is, in most studies, obtained in similar production circumstances and it is therefore more likely to relate to actual unpaid work output than in wage-based evaluations.

4.3 Non-cash benefits and bride price

Two more methods of assigning an imputed value on unpaid labour inputs are to be mentioned.

Non-cash benefits, i.e. the cost of daily keep in the village, were used in:

Africa

    United Republic of Tanzania 1973 (Macpherson and Jackson, 1975)

in order to establish the comparative costs of intermediate and village technologies of supplying water and shelling maize.

The authors comment that it is debatable whether the value of daily keep should be imputed when there is "surplus labour", that is when the labour time has no alternative productive use.

The bride price, i.e. the sums paid to the bride herself, excluding any payments to the bride's parents, was used in:

Africa

    Nigeria 1950-51 (Prest and Stewart, 1953)

for determining an approximate value of domestic activities in national accounting.

The authors comment that this evaluation method may be controversial: it undervaluates domestic activities because various annual payments are not counted and it does not account for the domestic activities performed by husbands and children.

4.4 Conclusions on input-related evaluations

The evaluations reviewed in this chapter assess the value of domestic and related activities by imputing a value to unpaid labour inputs.

The results which can be obtained with this approach were illustrated with a selection of studies relying on relatively large sample surveys, or derived from anthropological observations of a minimum of 100 households and controlled for seasonal variations.

One of the conclusions which can be drawn from the studies at hand is that the value of labour inputs into domestic activities is anything but negligible. For Mexico City's housewives alone, this value is equal to the contribution of the country's total agricultural sector to GDP (Rendón, 1979). The lowest evaluations in Venezuela are close to the value of the product of the petroleum sector and larger than the value of any other single economic sector (Valecillos et al., 1983).

General quantitative conclusions about the value of unpaid labour inputs into domestic activities cannot be drawn because of several methodological difficulties which were discussed in this chapter. Several quantitative observations can however be made. Macro-economic evaluations set the value of household labour inputs at a minimum of about 20 per cent and at a maximum of about 50 per cent of the national income. Household-level evaluations vary from about 40 per cent to 100 per cent of household monetary income. The lowest as well as the highest evaluations cover only part of the population involved in domestic activities (e.g. housewives only, or in one large city only, etc.) or cover only part of domestic activities.

Apart from the global results reported in this chapter, the summaries in Part II report other results obtained with evaluations based on the value of labour inputs. Several studies show the impact of higher income and of access to capital on returns to labour in non-monetary activities; they show how low returns to labour combine with long work schedules in the poorer households.

From the methodological point of view, the evaluations reviewed in this chapter testify to the problems encountered with the approach based on the value of labour inputs. They reveal the imaginative efforts deployed in the search for solutions. Only two methods, however, appear acceptable on theoretical grounds for estimating the value of domestic activities.

One of these two methods imputes to unpaid household labour the wages of qualified substitute household workers carrying household management responsibilities; in practice, however, paid substitute household workers may not be available (let alone workers with such qualification requirements) and the wages are therefore undetermined. The other method is to base the imputation on returns to labour in other activities, these returns having the advantage of being related to an actual output. In this approach, returns to market-oriented activities similar to domestic activities appear preferable; when such similar market activities do not exist, returns to labour in other non-monetary activities appear acceptable alternatives.

Wage-based evaluation methods reflect the structure of market wages; they are sensitive to labour market factors but are not sensitive to household production circumstances nor to household real output. An interesting illustration of this particularity is provided by the results obtained with different categories of wages applied to the same initial data basis in Venezuela (Valecillos et al., 1983): adults' inputs into domestic activities, in the ten largest cities, when expressed as a percentage of national income, are evaluated at:

22   per cent when based on wages of substitute household workers and average wages of females in service occupations;

32   per cent when based on wages for equivalent market functions;

41   per cent when based on average wages in their occupation for employed housewives and average wages of all female workers for housewives not in the labour force.

The lowest wages necessarily produce the lowest evaluations; female wages produce lower evaluations than male wages. As pointed out by Valecillos et al., 41 per cent is not a maximal evaluation for adults' inputs into domestic activities in Venezuela, as this figure still reflects the fact that women's wages are 59 per cent lower than men's.

All monetary evaluations of labour inputs have to rely on evaluations of the volume of labour inputs, expressed in number of workers or in time, with their problems (discussed in Chapter

3). The monetary evaluations do not tell more about the relative magnitude of labour inputs in the market and non-market sectors than the volume data on which they rely. The volume of inputs is the significant element in these evaluations: the values selected for the imputation (wages, returns to labour, or other) then act as coefficients reflecting the assumptions underlying their selection and the labour market factors bearing on them.

The value of labour inputs into domestic activities has sometimes been equated to value added in these activities and, as such, it has been compared to national income while it is only comparable to the item "compensation of employees" in the national accounts.

CHAPTER 5

OUTPUT-RELATED EVALUATIONS OF HOUSEHOLD PRODUCTION

This chapter reviews evaluations which take as a starting-point the output of household production and which are expressed either in physical or in monetary units, i.e. evaluations which measure either the volume or the value of household output.

5.1 Output-related evaluations: volume of output

The volume of household output was used for evaluating household production in:

Africa

    Cameroon 1964-74 (Henn, 1978)

Asia

    Bangladesh 1976-77 (Cain, 1977)

    Philippines 1975-76 (Ybañez-Gonzalo and Evenson, 1978)

Results

In southern Cameroon in 1964, Henn estimates that, for preparing the evening meals, rural women on the average carry home more than 2 tons of firewood annually.

In Bangladesh in 1976-77, Cain estimates that rural male children become net producers of calories at the latest by age 12.

In the Philippines in 1975-76, Ybañez-Gonzalo and Evenson estimate the production function of nutrients by households, by regressing the volume of household output (aggregate nutrient intake) on the value of household inputs: cooking time shows a high marginal value.

Methodological comments

Although interesting because they provide striking illustrations of household output, evaluations expressed in physical units cannot be aggregated and are therefore not usable for economic analysis or economic planning purposes.

5.2 Output-related evaluations: value of output

This section reviews evaluations which take as a starting-point household output and which express the results in monetary units, i.e. evaluations measuring the value of household product.

5.2.1 Gross output value and value added derived from consumer expenditures

This method derives the imputed value of household output from the value of intermediate consumption, i.e. from consumption expenditures for goods consumed in the production process. It was used in:

Latin America

Mexico, 1977 (Pedrero Nieto, 1983)

Pedrero Nieto first calculates the gross output of households' food preparation by applying a technical coefficient, borrowed from market enterprises (restaurants), to the value of raw materials consumed in the production process, i.e. to consumers' expenditures for food and beverages consumed in households. She then calculates value added by deducting the value of these raw materials from the gross output value.

Results

On this basis, Pedrero Nieto estimates that, in Mexico in 1977, this "rough evaluation" of the income in kind produced by one single household activity, namely food preparation, amounts to:

- a value larger or equal to their monetary income for the lower six income deciles of the population;
- and a value equal to half the monetary income for the highest decile of the population.

Methodological comments

The imputation of the technical coefficient of market enterprises to households is questionable because of productivity considerations. As discussed earlier (section 4.1.6, discussion of evaluations based on wages for equivalent market functions), households and market enterprises operate in different circumstances and there is every reason to believe that their "mix" of factor inputs is different.

5.2.2 Gross output value and value added derived from price of equivalent market product

The majority of output-related evaluations start with an estimate of the volume of household output and impute to it the price (a producer price or a retail price) of a market good or service considered equivalent to the household product. The value thus obtained is an imputed gross output value of household production. In some evaluations, intermediate consumption is deducted from the gross output value in order to determine the imputed value added.

In practice, gross output value and value added are not always clearly distinguishable in the evaluations under consideration. In subsistence activities, intermediate consumption and particularly the monetary component of intermediate consumption may be relatively small in comparison to gross output value; some authors therefore tend to neglect them. In this study, we classified under "value added" only the evaluations which specified that intermediate consumption was deducted. Differences between the two groups of evaluations, "gross output" and "value added" may be nominal in some cases.

In a similar way, in subsistence activities, the difference between "value added" and "returns to capital and labour" may be small. Dahl (1979) calculates the operating surplus (value added minus compensation to employees, consumption of fixed capital, and the excess of indirect taxes over subsidies), i.e. returns to capital and self-employed labour. In rural Botswana in 1974-75, he finds the operating surplus for various activities to be as follows in percentages of value added in the same activity:

gathering   100 per cent,
hunting and fishing   96 per cent,
manufacturing   90 per cent.

No attempt is made, in the studies under consideration, to separate the respective shares of capital and of labour in these returns. As an empirical approximation, perhaps derived from households' own perception, "returns to capital and labour" are handled as "returns to labour". The positive relation between capital ownership and returns to labour per hour of work, in market-oriented activities similar to household non-monetary activities, is illustrated by several studies: for instance, by Nag, White, and Peet (1978), in Java, for agriculture and food processing (ownership of land, of plough animals), and for trade (bicycle ownership); by Longhurst (1982), in Nigeria, for cooking food for sale (investment in raw foods yielding higher returns). Evers (1984) calls attention to the positive relation between capital ownership and returns to labour in non-market production in urban Indonesia. He observes that in Jakarta in 1979, for low-income households, access to land and resources and to capital equipment for domestic activities (sewing machines, stoves, bicycles, etc.) appear to be as important for household own-account production and survival as the composition of the household labour force or the proportion of dependants (children and old people) to adult household members.

Gross output value of domestic or related activities was determined on the basis of market prices, in:

Africa
         Cameroon 1964-74 (Henn, 1978)

Asia
         Indonesia 1975-76 (Hart, 1980)
         Indonesia 1979 (Evers, 1981a and b)
         Malaysia 1976-77 (Kusnic and Da Vanzo, 1980)

Latin America
         Bolivia 1983 (Tellería Geiger, 1983)

Oceania
         Papua New Guinea 1960-74 (Papua New Guinea, 1974)

Fisk (1975b) recommends use of gross output value at price of equivalent market product for the evaluation of subsistence income in the national accounts of the Pacific region.

Value added in domestic or related activities was derived from gross output value at price of equivalent market product, in:

Africa
         Botswana 1974-75 (Botswana, 1976; Dahl, 1979)
         Lesotho 1976 (Feachem et al., 1978)
         Nigeria 1950-51 (Prest and Stewart, 1953)

Asia
         Lebanon 1980 (Lorfing and Khalaf, 1985)
         Nepal 1980 (Acharya and Bennett, 1981 and 1983)
         Pakistan 1975-76 (Alauddin, 1980)

Dommen (1974), discussing accounting procedures in South Pacific economies, recommends value added derived from gross output value at the price of an equivalent market product, for the evaluation of non-monetary income generated in collecting firewood, manufacturing for own-consumption, and so on.

Results

In the evaluations under review, the volume of household output was imputed the price of an equivalent market product for determining the value of own-account production in the following activities: hunting and fishing; firewood and other fuel collection and preparation; water collection; food processing; wild food gathering; manufacturing (building materials, furniture, farm tools, clothes, woven materials, canoes, cooking utensils, etc.); transportion; health care. Not all studies include all these activities, nor do they all show the imputed value separately from the value of other subsistence activities.

Except for national accounts evaluations, studies do not claim that their samples are representative of the whole population. However, several authors consider their studies to be representative of a sizeable fraction (about 70-80 per cent) of the population or representative of typical segments of the population; results selected from these studies are presented here as illustrations, valid, however, only for the particular activities and for the particular socio-economic and cultural circumstances under consideration.

In rural Botswana in 1974-75, Dahl, in a macro-economic evaluation, makes estimates that hunting and fishing accounted for 2.6 per cent, firewood and wild food collection for 6.6 per cent, and part of manufacturing for 0.1 per cent of the value of subsistence production exclusive of water fetching, of domestic activities, and of part of manufacturing. (Subsistence production accounts for 58 per cent of total rural value added.)

In rural southern Cameroon in 1974, we calculate from Henn's household level estimates that firewood collection accounts for 8.4 per cent, and household goods and housing for 5 per cent of the gross output value of subsistence production, exclusive of water fetching and of domestic activities. (Subsistence production accounts for 54 per cent of total household income, i.e. cash plus subsistence incomes.) <u>Domestic activities</u>, estimated by her on the basis of returns to labour in subsistence and market-oriented activities (see section 4.2), <u>add another 30 per cent to household income</u>. From her data, we calculate that subsistence income inclusive of domestic activities accounts for 65 per cent of grand total household income (i.e. cash income, plus subsistence income, plus domestic activities).

In rural Lesotho in 1976, Feachem et al. start from the capital cost of providing a typical water supply, for estimating the value of time spent by women in carrying water. They estimate that the expense forgone by carrying water, in the villages under consideration, sets the value of water-carrying time at 4 cents per hour. As a point of comparison, domestic servants in towns, doing similar work in other people's houses, are paid around 10 cents per hour.

In urban Indonesia in 1979, Evers estimates that for the <u>kampong</u> dwellers of Jakarta, subsistence income (inclusive of water fetching, firewood collection and part of domestic activities) is equivalent to 18 per cent of the consumption expenditures. He stresses the strategic importance of own-account production for low-income households: in order to survive, half of the workers in the informal sector have to add to their monetary incomes more than 30 per cent in terms of non-monetary income.

In urban and rural Peninsular Malaysia in 1976-77, Kusnic and Da Vanzo estimate that, for the population under study, the grand total income (cash income, plus subsistence income inclusive of domestic activities) is as follows:
- at the mean, 56 per cent higher than cash income;
- at the median, more than 100 per cent higher than cash income;
- at the mean, for the poorest decile of the population, over 360 per cent higher than cash income.

In rural Nepal in 1980, Acharya and Bennett estimate for the villages under consideration, hunting and gathering account for 4.8 per cent, manufacturing (including sewing) for 1.9 per cent, and food processing for 15.6 per cent of the production performed on the household premises; of this production which accounts for 81.4 per cent of household income, 14.8 per cent is sold. (Subsistence income, exclusive of domestic activities and of water fetching, accounts for 70 per cent of total household income.)

In urban Pakistan in 1975-76, Alauddin estimates that the domestic activities (partly evaluated on the basis of wages of substitute household workers, see section 4.1.1) of the female population of Lahore produced:
- at the macro-economic level, a value-added equivalent to approximately 35 per cent of GNP;
- at the household level, on average for the sample under consideration, an additional income in kind equivalent to approximately 38 per cent of households' cash income, i.e. approximately 28 per cent of grand total household income (cash income plus subsistence income inclusive of domestic activities).

On the basis of Alauddin's data, we calculated average values per income group. The monthly average value of women's domestic activities in the sample is:
- Rs.315 for households with a monthly cash income of Rs.100-500, i.e. more than 100 per cent of the average cash income of Rs.300;
- Rs.930 for households with a monthly cash income of Rs.3,000-4,000, i.e. 27 per cent of the average cash income of Rs.3,500.

The absolute value of domestic activities thus appears to rise steadily with cash income, while their share in total income decreases steadily as cash income increases.

Methodological comments

Selection of market prices. The selection of market prices for evaluating non-market output touches upon a controversial question for which general agreement has not yet been reached: Should producer prices or retail prices be used for the imputation? Blades (1975) and Fisk (1975a and b) discuss the problem at length in relation to the valuation of agricultural subsistence product in the national accounts of developing countries. They both stress the relation between the purpose pursued by the evaluation and the selection of the one or the other category of prices. The conclusions they reach differ more in appearance than in substance.

Blades' conclusion is that "although there is clearly no single 'correct' solution for all purposes ... producer rather than retail prices best serve the kind of purposes for which national accounts are most commonly used, namely analysis of the structure and growth of production" (Blades, 1975, pp. 59-62). This opinion is in agreement with the SNA recommendation that own-account output be valued at producers' prices on the ground that they "furnish a measure of the income forgone, or the costs incurred, in consuming the commodities and assign the proper weight to the output as compared to marketed products" (United Nations, Statistical Office, 1968, paragraph 6.21). Blades does however allow for the possibility that in many situations retail prices will be the correct measure of income forgone. This will occur, for example, when farmers have no opportunity of selling their produce at the farm gate but must sell it themselves on a retail basis in nearby markets: the retail price would then accurately measure the income forgone in the farmer's decision to consume his crops rather than sell them.

Fisk's conclusion is that –

... the valuation at retail prices will be the appropriate measure for the main purposes [of national accounting] ... However, it is not asserted that this is necessarily the best measure for all national income purposes. There may be a need for estimates based on producers' prices also; but where this is so, these should be presented in addition to, and not instead of, those based on market prices (Fisk, 1975b, p. 278).

Blades and Fisk differ essentially only on which purposes are to be considered the main purposes of the SNA.

The SNA calls on a micro-economic concept, "income forgone", related to the production account and recommends the use of producer prices. "Expense forgone", a concept related to the consumption account, provides an alternative way of looking at the value of goods consumed by the producer; in this approach retail prices (purchaser prices) are appropriate. The selection of the income forgone or expense forgone approach of producer or retail prices depends on the purpose of the evaluation, i.e. on whether one is interested in the production account or in the consumption account. But within the production account, it also depends on whether one is interested in the "structure of production" at one point in time (i.e. in the relative contribution of the various sectors to the total sum of goods and services available) or in the "growth of production" (i.e. in changes, over a time span, in the volume of production); this aspect, particularly clear in relation to domestic activities, is discussed below. The problems encountered in price selection illustrate one of the difficult decisions to be taken in the revision of the SNA: how to construct a coherent accounting system that would meet the different purposes pursued by its users.

In the case of domestic activities, the same problems arise: Should they be valued at producers' prices or at retail prices? Again, the solution depends on the purpose of the evaluation. If the purpose is to assess, at the micro-economic level, the total income available to households, the evaluation should be at retail prices, i.e. through the expense forgone approach. This amounts to saying that, for a household, the value of the goods and services it produces is equal to the cash it would have to disburse in order to purchase their market substitutes.

At the macro-economic level, the situation is more complex. If the purpose is to monitor the "growth" of production in order to determine if the total amount of marketed and own-production goods (let us say laundered clothes) available to the population for the satisfaction of its needs is increasing, then the evaluation should be performed at retail prices. The reason is the following. Over the time span during which growth is being measured, part of own-account production might be transferred to the market sector; for an identical <u>volume</u> of product (laundered clothes) transportation and distribution costs, commercial margins, taxes, and so on will be incurred and included in retail prices. If producer prices had been used after the transfer, national income data would be inflated with these costs and would erroneously give the impression of growth, while the actual volume of product available for consumption would have remained constant.

Still at the macro-economic level, if the purpose is to assess the actual flow of goods and services produced, then the evaluation of domestic activities should be performed at producer prices. Domestic productive activities do not generate transportation or distribution flows, commercial margins or taxes: retail prices would not be appropriate. This does not deny the possibility of performing comparisons over a time span in which own-account production is valued at producer prices and market production is valued at retail prices. But the interpretation of such comparisons requires caution: the observable "growth" does not correspond to an increase in the volume of product available to households; it corresponds to an increase of the productive activities required for making the product available to households.

For the evaluation of domestic activities, as for the evaluation of other non-monetary activities, the problem is then how to reconcile the divergent uses to be made of the evaluation results. Solutions to this problem probably have to be sought along the following lines: maximum clarity about which category of prices was selected, and, if at all possible, separate presentation of results derived from both categories of prices.

Producer prices are difficult to determine for domestic products because households do not keep detailed production accounts giving the value of intermediate consumption and of fixed capital consumption. In addition, the value of labour inputs is unknown and an imputation on the basis of market wages is not recommended because of the difficulties discussed in Chapter 4. Retail prices, because they are more easily observable and because they include the value of labour inputs, appear as a more practicable choice than producer prices for the evaluation of domestic activities.

The selection of market prices, in addition to the theoretical problems just discussed, also requires that choices be made, in practice, between prices which differ from area to area, from rural to urban markets and from one season to another, and so on. The SNA in general and authors dealing more specifically with non-monetary activities (Dommen, 1974, pp. 20-21; Fisk, 1975b, pp. 278-279) provide guide-lines on the handling of these choices, guide-lines applicable also to domestic and related activities.

Imputation of current market prices. For aggregate-level evaluations, the soundness of using current market prices which are linked to the current structure of production is sometimes questioned. Some authors have expressed concern about what the prices would be if all non-market output were sold. The point raised is similar to the one discussed above (see section 4.1.5) in relation to market wages. It calls for a similar reply: the assumption that all non-market output be sold is not necessary for evaluation purposes; the value of non-market household output at one point in time and space is related to the structure of production at that point and not to the prices pertaining to another structure of production. This point of view is shared by Blades when, commenting on Johnson's (1961) and Ward's (1971) discussion of this concern, he states:

> Speculation on these lines, however, is not really very fruitful. The prices which would prevail if all presently unexchanged output were sold would apply by definition to a highly specialised economy, and it is not obvious that such prices are in any way appropriate for valuing transactions in the unspecialised economies we are dealing with here (Blades, 1975, p. 59).

Exchange value vs. value to the consumer. For the economic measurement of market product, the convention, accepted for lack of a better alternative, is to equate "value" with exchange value, i.e. with price. Actual value to the consumer is not measured in economics; free consumers, assisted by market mechanisms, are assumed to manage an equilibrium between the value to them of the goods purchased and the price they accept to pay.

The economic evaluation of non-monetary activities draws attention to the conventional character of the equation: value equals exchange value. The value to the consumer of a subsistence commodity may remain unchanged even if its exchange value, under the pressure of market circumstances, undergoes large fluctuations. For instance, the imputed (exchange) value of a subsistence staple food may drop because of the arrival on urban markets of imported foods, while its value for the rural producer/consumer, i.e. its aptitude to meet nutrition needs, remains unchanged. Exchange value is strongly influenced by the structure of market prices and does not carry a simple relationship to value to the consumer. How then can one value a subsistence crop that producers cannot sell although they can feed upon it? For instance, how can one value a crop which is at full maturity, a quality for the consumer but a prohibitive characteristic for commercial purposes because it will have spoiled before it reaches the market? Or how can one value a crop with a small defect which impairs its market value but not its nutritional value for the producer-consumer?

These subsistence agriculture examples are but an introduction to the more difficult problem raised by domestic activities for which there is no market substitute. In some economies, the imputed exchange value of domestic activities measured at production cost is low because the exchange value of the labour they require is low. In such economies, the market usually does not provide substitute products; the performance of domestic activities is then <u>indispensable</u> for the functioning of all other economic sectors because their workers need meals, washed clothes, a dwelling in which to rest, and so on. What is, in such circumstances, the value of domestic activities? Is it infinite?

The purpose of this discussion is to draw attention to the limits of what is called value, limits which are not particular to domestic activities but which domestic activities help delineate in a particular way. It would be wrong to infer from the discussion that domestic activities cannot be evaluated and that they might as well be ignored.

<u>Advantages of evaluations imputing market prices on household output</u>. Evaluations imputing market prices on household output have the advantage, over other evaluation methods, of accounting for the production circumstances in which households operate. Also, because they are established along the same principles as national accounts, evaluations of value added in domestic and related activities yield results which are comparable to macro-economic evaluations of overall economic activity.

These output-related evaluations avoid several problems pertaining to evaluations based on time inputs, more precisely to wage-based evaluations.

In wage-based evaluations, it is necessary to distinguish between work and leisure in order to impute a value (wage) only to work time (3.3 and 4.1.5, volume of labour inputs). In the output-related approach, what matters is the output, regardless of whether it is the outcome of unpleasant or pleasant work, or of productive leisure; utility derived from the performance of the activity does not raise a problem as it does in wage-based evaluations.

Another problem avoided with the output-related approach is the handling of simultaneous activities. Wage-based evaluations take as a starting-point the volume of labour inputs, usually measured in time. In order to avoid double-counting of time, only one activity can be assigned to each unit of time; when several activities are performed simultaneously, only one of them can be accounted for in the evaluation. Output-related evaluations can account for all outputs regardless of whether they were produced simultaneously or in sequence.

When households sell part of the output of a particular activity and consume another part, the distinction between production time which is market oriented and production time which is for own-consumption raises a problem in wage-based evaluations. In output-related evaluations, however, it is possible to measure the two quantities separately.

Work intensity, another unresolved problem of wage-based evaluations, is avoided in output-related evaluations. In the former, it is questioned, for instance, whether the same wages should be imputed to children's work time as to adults' work time on the ground that children's output may be lower than that of adults. The matter is automatically resolved when measuring output directly.

Output-related evaluations do not require problematic assumptions about decision-making processes on household resources allocation. They therefore avoid the social and cultural biases introduced by evaluations based on opportunity cost of time.

5.3 Conclusions on output-related evaluations

The evaluations reviewed in this chapter take as a starting-point the output of domestic and related activities and determine their volume or their value.

The volume of household output was found to be used only sporadically and in a limited way as a method per se of evaluating domestic activities. On the other hand, it is the starting-point of all estimates of the value of household output.

With one exception where the evaluation is based on consumer expenditures, estimates of the value of household output are based on the price of goods and services produced in the market and equivalent to those produced in the household. In addition to non-monetary activities usually covered in the national accounts, these output-related evaluations cover domestic-related activities such as gathering of wild fruit and firewood, water collection, manufacturing of household goods of which no part is sold in the market, care of dwelling and home repairs, and some domestic activities. Domestic activities which are not evaluated on the basis of output (because of lack of data on its volume or because there are no equivalent market products providing a value) are sometimes evaluated on the basis of labour inputs.

As with all other studies reviewed in this volume, the results achieved with these evaluations are only valid for the socio-cultural and economic context in which the data were collected. With this reservation in mind, the studies under consideration yield some orders of magnitude about which the following overview can be given:
- subsistence activities, exclusive of domestic activities, amount in some rural areas (Botswana, Cameroon, Nepal) to 60 per cent of total rural value added and 54-70 per cent of total household income; domestic activities contribute another 30 per cent to household income;
- subsistence activities of the kampong dwellers, inclusive of part of domestic activities, amount in the urban area of Jakarta to 18 per cent of household monetary income;

- subsistence activities, inclusive of all domestic activities, amount in urban and rural Malaysia to <u>56 per cent of household monetary income</u>;
- domestic activities of females, in the urban area of Lahore, amount to <u>38 per cent of household monetary income</u> and 35 per cent of the nation's GNP.

It can be safely concluded from the evaluations at hand that subsistence activities, and among them domestic activities, generate a substantial part of income.

Some of the studies give indications on how the above-mentioned gross averages vary with household monetary income. These results are of interest from the point of view of income distribution, particularly when the study relates the value of output to time inputs: Kusnic and Da Vanzo (1980) show that in order to achieve their total income level, the poorer households have to resort to longer work-days than households with high monetary incomes. Evers (1981) shows that, because of better access to land and to other productive resources, the total value of subsistence income increases with growing household monetary income, while its relative value declines. We obtain a similar result with Alauddin's data. Evers' study in Indonesia and Henn's (1978) in Cameroon illustrate the difficulty of reproducing with urban wages the rural standard of living in urban centres deprived from access to subsistence activities.

From the point of view of its application, the evaluation method imputing market prices to household output raises some technical problems: determination of the volume of household output, selection of equivalent market products and determination of their market prices. These problems, however, are not particular to own-account household production. They have already been encountered and have, to a certain extent, been dealt with in national accounting.

The output-related method avoids several unresolved problems of wage-based evaluations like, for instance, those relative to the handling of simultaneous activities. While wage-based evaluations closely reflect the structure of market wages, output-related evaluations are less directly affected by wages although a wage component is present here too, incorporated in the market price. On the other hand, output-related evaluations are sensitive to the price-structure of the economy, i.e. to productivity factors and to the laws of supply and demand.

From the methodological point of view, the imputation of market prices to household output presents advantages over other evaluation methods: it accounts for household production circumstances and for real household output, its results are comparable to macro-economic evaluations of overall economic activity (national accounts), and, at the household level, it yields a value (value added) perceived as "expense forgone", a meaningful concept in economies with a low degree of monetisation where monetary resources give access to goods and services not otherwise available.

CHAPTER 6

GENERAL CONCLUSIONS

The evaluations reviewed in the preceding chapters deal with domestic and related activities; these activities are so similar to other own-account productive activities that the boundary drawn between them by official statistical definitions appears somewhat arbitrary. For instance, the borderline between meal preparation (a domestic activity) and food processing is rather tenuous: both are part of a chain of inter-related activities starting with subsistence agricultural production, including among others fuel and water collection, and ending with the final consumption of food compatible with human biology, personal tastes and social values. Although similar in nature and purpose, these activities are not handled in the same way in economic accounting: subsistence agriculture, food processing and fuel collection are recommended for inclusion in official statistics while meal preparation and water collection are not. For positioning the production boundary, statisticians rely on several criteria (see section 2.2): one of them is that the activity under consideration should make a significant contribution to the well-being of the population; another criterion is that the activity should raise no marked difficulty of measurement.

6.1 Economic evaluations of domestic and related activities

At the outset of this study, a number of questions were asked. Firstly, does the economic evaluation of domestic and related activities raise unusual and insurmountable difficulties of measurement, or is it possible to achieve evaluations compatible with economic accounting practice? Secondly, what are the orders of magnitude at stake, i.e. what are the relative contributions of market-oriented activities, of own-account productive activities and, among the latter, of domestic activities to final total consumption? Thirdly, is it desirable to perform systematic evaluations of domestic activities?

6.1.1 Feasibility

This review presented some 40 evaluations of domestic and related activities, evaluations displaying several imaginative innovations for solving the problems encountered.

From the methodological point of view, <u>output-related</u> <u>evaluations</u> and, more specifically, evaluations of <u>value added</u> <u>derived from the prices of equivalent market products</u> appear preferable to other approaches because they relate to actual household product and to household production circumstances. This method, which is the basic evaluation method in national accounting, consists of:

a. estimating the volume of household output in the various domestic activities;

b. valuing this output at a market price (either the price of the same good or service produced in the household and sold to outsiders, or the price of an equivalent good or service produced in the market);

c. deducting intermediate consumption (consumption expenditures for intermediate goods or market value of own-production goods consumed in the production process).

For activities where it is not possible to perform an output-related evaluation, but only for those (usually household activities producing goods or services for which there is no market equivalent product), it is necessary to resort to an <u>input-related evaluation</u>. This complementary method consists of:

a. estimating the volume of labour inputs (usually expressed in labour time);

b. assigning this input a market value which, in order of preference and depending on data availability, can be:

  b.1 the net returns to labour (exclusive of intermediate consumption) in market-oriented activities performed by the household and similar or even identical to domestic activities;

  b.2 the net returns to labour in other non-monetary productive activities for which output-related evaluations can be performed;

  b.3 the wages of polyvalent household workers (inclusive of income in kind) adjusted for skill level and managerial responsibilities.

The two first values (net returns to labour) are output-related and are imputed to labour inputs. The third value is to be used as a last resort method because it is exclusively input-related: it only gives the market value of labour inputs.

In practice, the performance of output-related evaluations requires an estimate of household output, the evaluation of intermediate consumption and the determination of market prices. These requirements are not without problems. Experience has, however, already been gained in solving similar problems in national accounting, in labour force statistics, in the calculation of cost-of-living indexes, and so on. If household survey data and micro-data sets are used, the difficulties connected with the economic evaluation of domestic and related activities should not appear any more insurmountable than those which have already been solved for other economic measurements.

At the household level, value added measures the net income in kind generated by household non-market activity; it measures a forgone expense. At the macro-economic level, value added measures an income in kind which escapes national accounting. For this reason, domestic activities are sometimes included in the "hidden economy". In fact, they are just about as "hidden" as is a child pulling on to his face a cloth that prevents him from seeing. Domestic activities have little in common with the market-oriented activities also categorised as hidden, usually concealed or illegal activities. Nor do domestic activities have much in common with the market-oriented "informal sector" with which they are sometimes associated.

Domestic activities, because they are fully non-market (both their inputs and outputs are non-market), require special evaluation techniques similar to those used for other non-market activities like subsistence agriculture. The value added by domestic activities is sufficiently "significant" to justify that they be handled in their own right, with special consideration for their own evaluation problems which are different from those raised by concealed, illegal or informal sector monetised activities. Domestic activities are the production side of the household sector, a sector usually acknowledged only for its role in "final consumption", consumption which, in fact, is largely intermediate consumption.

It would be most interesting to evaluate domestic activities by combining two complementary approaches: the measurement, in time units, of labour inputs and the assessment of value added generated in non-market household production. From these two sets of values, the returns to labour in non-market household production can be determined. Their comparison with returns to labour in market-oriented activities and, among others, their comparison with market wages would give an image of economic productivity (all factors productivity) in the household respective to productivity in the market.

6.1.2 Orders of magnitude

As pointed out by several authors, the production of cash crops, the operation of industrial plants and the performance of all market-oriented activities presuppose that certain basic needs be satisfied which are met by non-market productive activities. The share of final income to be credited therefore, at the national or household level, to non-market productive activities and, among them, to domestic and related activities is probably best illustrated by the proportion of total labour they require. This illustration is achieved by evaluations of the volume of labour inputs.

Because of their diversity, the evaluations reviewed in the present study do not permit one to draw any firm conclusion as to the time required for labour force activities and for domestic activities respectively. However, subject to all the reservations made earlier in this volume, for the populations under consideration, the order of magnitude of the time devoted to domestic and related activities is about 40-45 per cent of total labour time, a "significant" portion of the scarce resource human labour.

However, because not all labour time produces the same returns, it is, for some purposes, necessary to determine what are the returns to labour in various activities. Returns to labour can be measured in physical units: for instance, the amount of cereals ground in one hour by workers utilising different techniques can be measured and compared. Nutritive value, at the final consumption stage, can be measured in physical units for assessing the respective merits of different grinding and storage techniques. But if one wants to assess whether it "pays" (a value-related concept) to use one specific technique which is more costly than another, physical units are not adequate for answering the question. Nor do physical units permit overall assessment of economic activity as it is not possible to aggregate, nor even to compare in any meaningful way, outputs such as tons of copper, tons of rice, litres of water, and number of children cared for.

The practice in economics is then to measure returns to labour in monetary units, and the widely accepted convention is to measure these returns at the exchange value of the goods and services produced. Even for goods exchanged in the market, exchange value is not an entirely satisfactory measuring tool as it inadequately reflects value to the consumer. To impute an exchange value to goods and services produced by households for their own consumption may lead to an understatement of their actual economic value to the consumer (in terms of needs satisfaction) and to an understatement of final consumption.

Monetary evaluations also fail to assess the indispensability of some domestic activities and the indirect contribution of domestic activities to market-oriented economic activity. The indispensability of domestic productive activities is highest in rural societies where market substitutes are rare if not totally non-existent. However, it is precisely in these societies that an abundant labour supply tends to depress the wages and the prices paid for locally produced goods and services, therefore entailing low evaluations of non-market productive activities.

In spite of all these drawbacks, monetary evaluations provide some quantitative assessment of the relative importance of domestic activities in the overall productive effort towards the fulfilment of human needs, albeit a minimal assessment because of the points discussed in the two preceding paragraphs.

The evaluations reviewed in this study indicate that, even at this minimal assessment, domestic and related activities appear to produce a "significant" fraction of the goods and services consumed.

Wage-based evaluations of domestic activities give values ranging between 25 and 50 per cent of the national income. The range of values is inherent to the evaluation method itself and it reflects the structure of market wages. At the household level, in Latin America, it is estimated that domestic activities add an income in kind ranging from one-third to one-half of households' monetary income (ILO, Regional Office for Latin America and the Caribbean, 1984, p. 3).

Output-related evaluations are, at present, only a few. They give indications about the orders of magnitude at stake for the populations under study. The value of domestic activities performed in one single urban area (Lahore) is estimated at 35 per cent of the nation's GNP and at 38 per cent of households' monetary income. In some rural areas (Cameroon, Nepal) it is estimated that domestic activities add 30 per cent to total (monetary plus subsistence) household income. For the poorest households, the income in kind generated by own-account productive activities appears not only as a significant contribution to their total income, but actually as a matter of survival.

6.1.3 Desirability

The absence of quantitative evaluations of some non-monetary productive activities, in particular the absence of quantitative evaluations of domestic and related activities may have contributed to the failure of policies to account for these activities. The evaluations reviewed in this study do not provide values valid the world over. They do however yield orders of magnitude indicating that, when monitoring economic activity, economic development, or the utilisation of the scarce resource, labour, it would be sensible to monitor also all facets of the non-market sector including the significant contribution of domestic activities. Either national income and labour force definitions can be broadened so as to reflect the overall non-market sector, or new concepts and accounting procedures have to be developed for this purpose.

Let us take a few examples. The figures provided in several studies draw a picture of people working long days of which only part is devoted to market-oriented activities; such people are "underemployed" while "overworked". Based on limitative definitions of the concept "labour" or "work", some employment policies, in particular some of those intended for women, assume the existence of a labour surplus which is not confirmed by time-use data. Simply to raise monetary income by providing job opportunities that increase the market workload without reducing the non-market workload is damaging from the point of view of welfare.

Because they disregard a sizeable fraction of non-market productive activity, economic development policies too often disregard the necessity of acting simultaneously on the generation of monetary income and on the production of market substitutes for non-market goods and services. For many women, given their total hours of work, increased participation in the monetised sectors of the economy will result in improved standards of living only if part of the monetary income thus earned can be - and actually is - used for reducing the workload in the least productive of their non-market activities.

If economic development is to produce a net increase in welfare, in addition to considering the impact of new technologies (in market-oriented activities) or the impact of new job opportunities on the distribution of income, it also is necessary to consider their impact on the distribution of the workload between various categories of the population (men/women; migrants/sedentaries; urban/rural). Because they utilise limitative definitions of "income" and of "labour", economic development policies often disregard the costs of economic growth, both in increased labour time and in forgone non-market income for some categories of the population.

Just as statisticians and policy-makers tend to recognise as economic only those activities which are monetised, individuals tend to neglect the monetary value of non-monetary activities. This is partly the result of the fascination exerted by high technology products only available in exchange of money. It is also partly due to the absence of market substitutes for household-produced goods and services, substitutes that would provide alternatives for the use of monetary income. And finally, the low interest accorded to the economic value of domestic and other non-monetary activities may have some relation with their apparent low productivity levels: a vicious circle because this low productivity is tied to the attribution of the poorer lands to subsistence agriculture, to the concentration of capital in cash-crop production, and to the lack of technical skills and political determination at the community level for servicing improved equipment for domestic and related activities. The economic undervaluation of non-monetary productive activities has consequences for the economic and social status of those performing them. Formal recognition of the economic value of all these activities, including that of domestic and related activities, and official measurements of this value, may contribute to reversing these trends.

6.2 Future steps

Third World countries are pressing for a better coverage of non-monetary activities in the national accounts, because the unsatisfactory aspects of present SNA coverage are more easily apparent in their economies. However, even in industrialised countries, SNA coverage is an object of concern: as early as the 1920s, national accountants were concerned by the absence of domestic activities in economic accounts; sporadic evaluations were performed ever since.

These evaluations yield, for domestic activities in industrialised countries, average values of 40-50 per cent of the

GNP. These values should not be compared to those obtained in Third World countries with output-related evaluations because the great majority of the evaluations performed in industrialised countries are input related. (In spite of the fact that output-related evaluations of domestic activities would be easier to achieve in highly monetised economies where market substitutes are available for a wide range of domestic activities, this approach has only recently begun to be used in industrialised countries.)

In order to monitor all "significant contributions" to total consumption, the evalation of domestic and related activities is a requirement to be met in all countries, no matter what their degree of monetisation. It would be a mistake to perform these evaluations only in Third World countries or, as is sometimes proposed, to limit the coverage there to those activities which are monetised in industrialised countries.

Evaluations of domestic and related activities are needed for two purposes:
- to be ready with data compatible with national accounting practice and which can be presented as building blocks, or in satellite accounts, or in any other form recommended in the forthcoming revision of the SNA;
- to provide reliable data for the many other uses (welfare policy, development policy, etc.) for which they are required.

The SNA is currently being revised with a mandate to try and expand the coverage of non-monetary activities. Women's organistions, the world over, are exerting political pressure for official statistics to reflect the so far unrecorded contributions of women to the economy. The moment seems appropriate for calling on international collaboration for defining evaluation guide-lines. Enough experience is now available for agreement to be reached on evaluation and data collection methodology. The present study and the earlier reviews (Goldschmidt-Clermont, 1982 and 1983b) show that, from the point of view of evaluation methodology, the validity - or lack of validity - of the different methods of imputing economic values to non-market activities is very similar across economies presenting differing degrees of monetisation. Furthermore, in different contexts, the weaknesses and advantages of the various methods are highlighted. For data collection too, mutual benefit can be derived from confronting differences and similarities; from the point of view of monetisation and market penetration, countries are situated on a continuum which is artifically broken down by official classifications. For all these reasons, it would appear valuable for those involved in the economic evaluation of domestic activities to set up a network for the exchange of information and experiences, and to pursue together, at regular intervals, the reflection on their common concerns.

The studies under review show that economic evaluations of domestic activities are feasible. The orders of magnitude at stake indicate that these evaluations are necessary. However, in order to achieve comprehensive and reliable evaluations, a sizeable statistical effort will be needed. This effort will appear relatively small in comparison with the effort already invested in official statistics, precisely because the evaluation of domestic activities can rely on the experience gained in market sector measurements. The problems can probably be solved and the results obtained at the cost of an effort less than proportional to the importance of domestic activities in the overall economy.

PART II

EVALUATION SUMMARIES

1. INTRODUCTORY REMARKS

Part II of this volume present excerpts from some 40 economic evaluations of domestic and related activities and of their related unpaid work inputs. The evaluations were performed in Africa, Asia, Latin America, and Oceania. A few words are required about content and presentation.

<u>Content</u>. It is a delicate task to try and compact into a few pages the work performed by others and their research results. The purposes pursued, the disciplines and methodologies used, the socio-economic and cultural situations observed differ greatly. Still, all the publications retained for this review have something to contribute towards the subject of this study: the exploration of the solutions adopted in particular cases, in order to meet the problems raised by the economic evaluation of non-market productive activities.

This concern – economic evaluation methodologies – guided the selection of data and quotations from the publications reviewed. What is presented here is therefore not really "summaries" of publications, but "research-oriented excerpts"; any selection is bound to involve subjective and arbitrary decisions. It is hoped that these excerpts will contribute to make existing research results more widely known and will encourage the reader to look up the original publications.

This review does not exhaust the supply of evaluations. It was not possible to secure all evaluations which had come to our attention. Others may have escaped our net. The subject is relatively new and, although approached in many disciplines, it is usually treated as a subsidiary theme only. As a result, standard bibliographic searches yield little information, and progress requires grapevine-like searches and networks.

One more word about content. Readers familiar with an earlier publication by the same author (1982) will notice that, although the emphasis remains on evaluation methodology, more room is given to the presentation of evaluation results. Under the pressure of widespread interest in the economic value of domestic and related activities, illustrative results were included; care should however be exercised in order to avoid misinterpretation of the data and particularly to avoid unjustified generalisations. As discussed in Part I, in the present state of knowledge, the results are to be regarded as mere illustrations of a particular research approach, in a particular context. Attempts at comparing results of different evaluations or extrapolations beyond the limits of the study under consideration would in most cases be unwarranted. The authors' warnings about the limitations of their data are quoted in the excerpts and should be respected.

<u>Presentation</u>. The 1982 monograph dealt with economic evaluations of unpaid household work performed mostly in Europe and North America, but also in Australia, Israel and Japan, between 1921 and 1981. Over this time span, evaluation methods

had evolved; a presentation in chronological order was therefore
adopted highlighting this evolution. In the present study, a
chronological presentation is not justified as the evaluations
reviewed here were performed over a much shorter period of time:
with one exception, they were all published between 1973 and 1985.

A geographical presentation seems more appropriate: the
evaluations are therefore grouped alphabetically, by continent
and by country; within a country, they are presented in
chronological order of period covered. (Access by authors is
possible by means of the synoptic presentation on pages 67-69).

Apart from this difference in the grouping of evaluations,
presentation is kept as close as possible to presentation in the
1982 monograph, so as to facilitate the reader's task of moving
from one to the other.

Each evaluation excerpt includes:
- geographical location of study, period covered, setting
  (urban or rural);
- author's name, date and title of publication (full
  references can be found in the bibliography at the end of
  the volume);
- purpose of the evaluation;
- evaluation methods used;
- selected evaluation results;
- comments relative to the particular evaluation under
  consideration (general comments on methodology appear in
  Part I).

2. SYNOPTIC PRESENTATION OF EVALUATIONS

Author(s)	Date of publication	Country and period covered	Evaluation methods*	Page
Acharya and Bennett	1981 and 1983	Nepal, 1980	I.t W.Ss and VA.PEM	143
Alauddin	1980	Pakistan, 1975-76	W.Ss and VA.PEM	150
Botswana, Ministry of Finance and Development Planning	1976	Botswana, 1974-75	W.M. and VA.PEM	73
Cabañero	1978	Philippines, 1975-76	R.O	156
Cain	1977 and 1980	Bangladesh, 1976-77	I.t O.a	109
Campiótti	1983	Uruguay, 1983	I.t	189
Dahl	1979	Botswana, 1974-75	W.M and VA.PEM	75
Evenson, Popkin and King-Quizon	1980	Philippines, 1975-77	I.t W.S W.OCT	162
Evers	1981	Indonesia, 1979	GO.PEM	125
Evers and Korff	1982	Thailand, 1980-82	I.t	168
Feachem et al.	1978	Lesotho, 1976	I.t VA.PEM	93
Gilbert Islands	1979	Kiribati and Tuvalu, 1972-74	W.M	195
Hart	1980	Indonesia, 1975-76	I.t R.O	119

* For meaning of abbreviations, see p. 70.

Author(s)	Date of publica-tion	Country and period covered	Evaluation methods*	Page
Henn	1978	Cameroon, 1964–74	O.a I.t R.O GO.PEM	84
King and Evenson	1983	Philippines, 1975–77	I.t W.OCT	166
King	1978	Philippines, 1975	W.OCT	154
Kritz et al.	1984	Argentina, 1983	I.t	170
Kusnic and Da Vanzo	1980	Malaysia, 1976–77	GO.PEM and W.OCT	138
Longhurst	1982	Nigeria, 1976	R.O	103
Lorfing and Khalaf	1985	Lebanon, 1980	W.S VA.PEM	135
Macpherson and Jackson	1975	United Republic of Tanzania, 1973	NCB	106
Martínez Espinoza	1983	Chile, 1983	I.t W.S and W.EMF W. OCT	177
Mueller	1984	Botswana, 1974–75	I.t R.O	79
Mukherjee	1983	India, 1970–71	R.O	116
Murray	1981	Lesotho, 1978	–	98
Nag, White and Peet	1978 and 1980	Indonesia and Nepal, 1972–73	I.t R.O	129

* For meaning of abbreviations, see p. 70.

SYNOPTIC PRESENTATION OF EVALUATIONS (concl.)

Author(s)	Date of publica- tion	Country and period covered	Evaluation methods*	Page
Navera	1978	Philippines, 1975-76	I.t	158
Papua New Guinea, Bureau of Statistics	1974	Papua, New Guinea, 1960-74	W.M GO.PEM	198
Pardo and Cruz	1983	Chile, 1981	I.t W.EMF W.OCT	174
Pedrero Nieto	1983	Mexico, 1970 1977, 1978	I.w W.Sp W.OCT GO.CE and VA.CE	183
Prest and Stewart	1953	Nigeria, 1950-51	BP VA.PEM	100
Rendón	1979	Mexico, 1970	W.Sp	182
Tellería Geiger	1983	Bolivia, 1983	I.t GO.PEM	172
Tueros, Hoyle and Kritz	1984	Peru, 1983	I.t	187
Valecillos et al.	1983	Venezuela, 1982	I.t W.OCT and W.Af W.S and W.Af W.EMF	192
Ybañez-Gonzalo and Evenson	1978	Philippines, 1975-76	W.OCT and O.a	160

* For meaning of abbreviations, see p. 70.

3. ABBREVIATIONS: ALPHABETICAL LISTING

BP	Bride price
GO.CE	Gross output value, derived from consumer expenditures
GO.PEM	Gross output value, at price of equivalent market product
I.t	Volume of labour inputs, in time
I.w	Volume of labour inputs, in workers
NCB	Value of non-cash benefits
O.a	Volume of output, by activity
R.O	Returns in other activities
VA.CE	Value added, derived from consumer expenditures
VA.PEM	Value added, at price of equivalent market product
W.A	Wage, average for all workers
W.Af	Wage, average for female workers
W.M	Wage, minimum
W.EMF	Wage, equivalent market function
W.OCT	Wage forgone or opportunity cost of time
W.S	Wage, substitute household worker
W.Sp	Wage, substitute household worker, polyvalent
W.Ss	Wage, substitute household worker, specialised

4. EVALUATION METHODS
AND RELATED ABBREVIATIONS

Inputs, volume

Volume of labour inputs, in time	I.t
Volume of labour inputs, in workers	I.w

Inputs, value

Wage, substitute household worker	W.S
Wage, substitute household worker, polyvalent	W.Sp
Wage, substitute household worker, specialised	W.Ss
Wage, equivalent market function	W.EMF
Wage forgone or opportunity cost of time	W.OCT
Wage, average for all workers	W.A
Wage, average for female workers	W.Af
Wage, minimum	W.M
Returns in other activities	R.O
Value of non-cash benefits	NCB
Bride price	BP

Output, volume

Volume of output, by activity	O.a

Output, value

Gross output value, derived from consumer expenditures on material inputs	GO.CE
Value added, derived from consumer expenditures on material inputs	VA.CE
Gross output value, at price of equivalent market product	GO.PEM
Value added, at price of equivalent market product	VA.PEM

BOTSWANA, Ministry of Finance and Development Planning, 1976

The Rural Income Distribution Survey in 1974-75

Purpose

To measure the statistical distribution of income among households in the rural areas, relative poverty, absolute poverty, the contributions of various sources of income to total household income, etc. (pp. 7-8).

Methods

Value added, at price of equivalent market product and minimum wages

Data on the volume of production (crops, cattle, game, fish, wild food, firewood, building materials, etc.) are collected from a representative sample of 1,800 households surveyed once a month over one year (pp. vi and 19).

Production for own consumption is valued at producers' selling prices averaged over the 12-month survey period (Central Statistical Office price lists, supplemented by special surveys, e.g. for edible wild plants). Expenses incurred in the production process are deducted for determining value added. (pp. 48; 56-59; 62-65; 201-210; 271-273; 291).

Labour contributed by household members in housebuilding is valued at the minimum rural wage for unskilled labour (p. 67).

Results

In the publication under review, incomes are shown by activity, without separating income derived from market-oriented activity and income derived from goods and services directly

---

* See also Botswana 2 and 3 for other studies using the same data base.

consumed in the household (pp. 201-202; 207; 271). These data were however collected separately for crop and animal husbandry, hunting, fishing, firewood collection and gathering edible wild plants (pp. 206-210 and 232-236); they should be available from the data base on magnetic tape.

Comment

For all rural households, any water gathered by the household or obtained from a communal tap was treated as having zero value, i.e. water gathering was throughout the analysis not treated as an income-producing activity (p. 105); nor were domestic activities (cooking, cleaning, laundering, shopping, care of children, etc.), repairing or improving hut and equipment, making floor, walls or yard of compound, processing food or making goods for own consumption, etc.

DAHL, 1979

Rural production in Botswana 1974/75: A national accounts analysis of the Rural Income Distribution Survey (RIDS)

Purpose

"To present a set of rural production accounts based on Botswana's Rural Income Distribution Survey (1976) data. ... To analyse them in terms of absolute flows, and not in terms of distributions of income, etc. as was done in the main RIDS publication" (Preface and p. 0/7).

Methods

RIDS data on rural economic activities is included and organised according to the United Nations System of National Accounts (United Nations, Statistical Office, 1968). For instance, subsistence production in manufacturing is included only if the household also sells the corresponding commodity.

Value added at price of equivalent market product and minimum wage

Production valued at market prices for crops, cattle, game, fish, wild food, firewood, building materials, etc.

Housebuilding on own account valued at minimum rural wage for unskilled labour.

For details on methodology, see Botswana 1, above.

---

* See also Botswana 1 and 3, for other studies using the same data base.

Results

The following table shows the relative value of rural production (monetary production and subsistence production exclusive of water collection, domestic activities and part of manufacturing) in relation to total GDP.

Total production in Botswana: Value added (VA) 1974-75

	(Thousands of Pula)		(Percentages)	
Rural economy				
Subsistence VA	53 574		23	58
Monetary VA[1]	38 345		17	42
Total rural VA		91 919	40	100
Rest of the economy		135 455	60	
Total GDP		227 374	100	

[1] Read "market transactions" as this item includes payments in kind as well as monetary transactions.

(Tables 3.2 and 3.3, p. 3/6)

"Thus the size of the rural economy is substantial, with a per capita value added from rural production at about Pula 130" (p. 0/1).

The next table (Rural production in Botswana) puts together data collected from several parts of H.-E. Dahl's publication, in order to show the relative economic importance of hunting and fishing, gathering and own-account construction, in relation to other productive activities.

Comments

"In RIDS, the production boundary is drawn widely, to include most non-market production activities, except for certain intra-household services like preparation of meals for (own) household consumption, child care, etc." (p. 4/3). (See Botswana 1, comment, above.)

Rural production in Botswana 1974-75, by production activity

Production activity	Crop husbandry	Animal husbandry	Manufacturing	Trading	Hunting, fishing	Gathering	Own-acct. construct.	Other activities[1]	Total, all activities
Gross output (GO)[2]									
Rural GO (P'000)	8 834	80 660	3 405	3 853	1 901	4 128	685	6 923	110 390
% of rural GO	8	73	3.1	3.5	1.7	3.7	0.6	6.3	100
Own consumption (OC)[3] (P'000)	6 349	42 716[4]	81	-	1 533	3 883	685	3 735	58 995
% of total OC	10.8	72.4	0.1	-	2.6	6.6	1.2	6.3	100
Value added (VA)[5]									
Rural VA (P'000)	7 988	65 211	2 413	3 309	1 893	4 128	655	6 292	91 889
% of rural VA	8.6	70.9	2.6	3.6	2	4.5	0.7	6.8	100
Own consumption[6] (P'000)	-	-	-	-	-	-	-	-	53 574[4]
% of rural VA	-	-	-	-	-	-	-	-	58
Operating surplus (OS)[7]									
Rural OS (P'000)	6 756	59 473[4]	2 175	2 623	1 828	4 128	563	1 093	78 639
% of rural OS	8.6	75.6	2.8	3.3	2.3	5.2	0.7	1.4	100
% of VA in same productive activity	84.6	91.2	90	79	96	100	85	17	85

1 "Home restaurants" (parties); real estate including owner-occupied housing; domestic servants; other services.
2 Table 1.12.1, p. 1/4. "Gross output equals quantity produced times price." (p. 4/4) 3 Table 1.12.2, p. 1/6.
4 Including about Pula 24 million increase in value of livestock herds: "Saving on hoof" (pp. 1/10 and 3/3). 5 Table
1.12.5, p. 1/12. "Value added equals gross output less [monetary] inputs for goods and services used" (p. 4/4). 6 Tables 3.2
and 3.3, p. 3/6. 7 Table 1.12.7, p. 1/14. "Operating surplus defined as value added less compensation to employees,
consumption of fixed capital and the excess of indirect taxes over subsidies" (p. 5/1) "[i.e.] remuneration of capital and return
to self-employed labour, e.g. as owners of cattle" (pp. 1/2 and 1/3). Balancing item of the production account.

"For countries where non-market economic activities are substantial, like Botswana, it is extremely difficult to measure the national income with acceptable accuracy without relying on a RIDS type of survey" (p. 0/5). "The Botswana Rural Income Distribution Survey probably constitutes a unique source of information for quantifying in great detail the pattern of non-marketed production and own-consumption in a developing country" (p. 0/8).

"The bulk of production activities other than cattle husbandry is carried out by households with less than 10 cattle, whose livestock production is only 17 per cent of total livestock production. [See original publication, for breakdown according to households' size of cattle holdings and mode of production (traditional, intermediate and modern).] Greater diversification goes with reduced cattle ownership. The fewer cattle, the less well off a household is. The less well off have to find their income bit by bit in many spheres" (p. 1/3). For instance, gathering represents 7 per cent of gross output for own consumption of traditional farmers and only 2 per cent for intermediate farmers (derived from table 1.12.2, p. 1/6).

The values for subsistence production (23 per cent of total GDP, 53 per cent of rural gross output and 58 per cent of rural value added) do not cover all subsistence production. They correspond only to the part of subsistence production which is recommended for inclusion in the national accounts (United Nations, Statistical Office, 1968).

Hunting, fishing, gathering and own-account construction combined account for:

6.0 per cent of rural gross output;
7.2 per cent of rural value added;
8.2 per cent of rural operating surplus;
10.4 per cent of rural gross output for own consumption.

These values come close to the values of production in crop husbandry (respectively 8, 8.6, 8.6 and 10.8 per cent).

Operating surplus covers remuneration of capital and returns to self-employed labour. It is an interesting concept for studying returns to unpaid labour when capital is nil (gathering, appendix table 1.4.20) or negligible (hunting and fishing, appendix table 1.3.20). Gathering is the "pure" case where value added and gross output are 100 per cent constituted of returns to labour. In hunting and fishing, returns to labour constitute 96 per cent of value added, and 91 per cent of gross output. It is therefore not surprising that, as noted by H.-E. Dahl, households with little or no access to capital resort to these production activities.

MUELLER, 1984

The value and allocation of time in rural Botswana

Purpose

To analyse the determinants – economic and institutional – of time allocation by rural households in Botswana and to consider some of the economic implications of time use patterns.

Methods

(a)   Volume of labour inputs, in time

Data are derived from the Rural Income Distribution Survey conducted by the Government of Botswana in 1975 (see Botswana 1, above). The time allocation data pertain to the day prior to the interview and were obtained only in five of the 12 monthly rounds, for all persons in the household (4,600 individuals) 6 years of age and above (pp. 330-331).

(b)   Returns in other activities

"The theoretical framework on which this paper is based assumes that time allocations are responsive to economic incentives. That is, they are expected to be sensitive to income and price-of-time (or productivity) effects. Methodologically, this paper differs from previous studies with a similar theoretical orientation in two respects.

---

* See also Botswana 1 and 2 for other studies using the same data base.

First, it attempts to estimate the marginal contribution to
income generation of family time inputs, disaggregated by
age and sex. Secondly, in view of the limited
opportunities for wage labour, in the time use analysis the
price of time is measured, not by market wages (actual or
estimated) but by the productivity of time in
self-employment as determined by inputs of human and
non-human capital plus such characteristics as age and
location" (p. 330). "For estimation purposes, household
income is assumed to be generated by a production function
where age/sex specific time, human capital (education) and
physical assets (land, cattle, smaller animals) are inputs.
... Marginal productivities of work time were calculated
from the regressions, assuming a 6-hour work day on the
average" (pp. 337 and 342).

Results

(a) The distribution of activity time of males and females by
age is given in the tables on the following pages.
"When the time use data are examined by season of the
year, it appears that men allocate about 60 per cent more
time to income earning activities during the busy than
during the slack season, and boys about 100 per cent more.
The seasonality of time use is even more pronounced for
women and girls because crop production is largely 'women's
work'. Housework time seems to be quite insensitive to the
seasonality in labour demand" (p. 333).

(b) "The marginal productivity of male labour comes to 0.18 to
0.22 Pula per day
and the marginal productivity of female labour is slightly
lower" (p. 342).
N.B.: These figures include income in kind, and relate only
to "income-earning activities [see tables] which contribute
to GNP" (p. 329).
The marginal productivity of labour can be compared
with daily average wages in rural areas (Lucas, 1981, table
7, p. 13).
1.26 Pula per day for men without education;
1.50 Pula per day for men with 1-4 years of schooling;
0.54 Pula per day for women with 0-4 years of education;
and with average daily income in rural areas:
0.35 Pula per person.

Distribution of activity time by age: Males

Activities	Age 7-9	10-14	15-19	20-29	30-39	40-49	50-59	60+	All males

Percentage distribution of total time

Activities	Age 7-9	10-14	15-19	20-29	30-39	40-49	50-59	60+	All males
Crop husbandry	2.1	3.0	3.5	5.2	6.1	9.1	7.7	10.5	5.4
Animal husbandry	22.3	28.8	23.9	12.5	15.1	10.6	12.3	9.2	18.7
Wage labour	0.4	0.4	2.0	12.2	8.1	7.4	5.5	1.9	4.0
Trading, vending, processing	0.1	0.1	0.7	0.9	1.0	1.9	1.1	1.6	0.8
Hunting or gathering	1.2	1.6	1.9	2.0	2.6	3.0	1.9	2.3	2.0
All income-earning activities	26.2	33.9	32.0	32.9	32.8	32.1	28.4	25.6	30.8
Repairing, new buildings	0.8	0.5	1.6	1.9	2.6	3.3	5.6	3.7	2.1
Fetching water	1.6	2.3	2.2	1.9	1.7	1.4	0.2	1.1	1.7
Child care	3.8	1.7	0.9	0.5	0.5	0.1	0.0	0.2	1.2
Housework[1]	2.8	4.4	5.1	5.2	3.0	4.0	2.2	2.4	3.8
All house-keeping activities	8.9	8.9	9.8	9.6	7.8	8.7	8.0	7.3	8.7
Schooling	11.1	13.7	9.3	1.1	0.3	0.6	0.3	0.1	6.1
Illness and health care	1.5	1.5	2.6	3.0	2.5	2.9	5.3	8.4	3.2
Meetings	0.0	0.0	0.1	0.4	1.3	2.0	2.7	2.9	0.9
Leisure	52.3	42.0	46.2	53.1	55.3	53.6	55.3	55.7	50.3
All non-work activities	53.8	43.5	48.8	56.5	59.1	58.5	63.2	67.0	54.4
All activities	100.0	100.0	100.0	100.0	100.0	100.0	100.0	100.0	100.0

[1] Includes cooking, stamping grain, cleaning, washing, shopping, making or processing goods for own consumption or use, e.g. beer, skins, dresses, pots, etc. (Botswana, 1976, p. 231).

(Table 1, p. 332)

Distribution of activity time by age: Females

Activities	Age 7-9	10-14	15-19	20-29	30-39	40-49	50-59	60+	All females
Percentage distribution of total time									
Crop husbandry	2.4	3.5	6.0	8.6	10.2	12.8	13.4	11.5	8.0
Animal husbandry	3.2	3.8	2.1	1.5	1.2	0.9	0.5	0.5	1.9
Wage labour	0.1	0.8	2.1	2.0	1.1	1.7	0.8	0.1	1.2
Trading, vending, processing	0.0	0.5	1.5	1.7	3.0	1.6	1.8	1.2	1.4
Hunting or gathering	1.6	2.6	2.8	2.5	2.7	2.5	2.8	2.3	2.5
All income-earning activities	7.2	11.2	14.4	16.4	18.1	19.5	19.2	15.6	15.0
Repairing, new buildings	0.5	0.8	2.2	3.2	4.3	5.5	5.8	4.9	3.1
Fetching water	4.8	6.3	7.7	7.8	7.4	6.4	5.8	4.4	6.5
Child care	10.5	5.5	3.4	6.2	3.5	1.9	1.5	1.5	4.5
Housework[1]	9.5	15.5	20.8	22.3	19.5	18.7	18.4	13.5	17.8
All house-keeping activities	25.3	28.3	34.1	39.5	34.7	32.6	31.5	24.3	32.0
Schooling	14.4	17.4	8.3	1.2	0.3	0.3	0.2	0.1	5.8
Illness and health care	1.1	2.0	3.6	4.6	5.6	6.3	6.4	8.6	4.5
Meetings	0.0	0.2	0.4	0.3	0.6	0.9	0.4	0.5	0.4
Leisure	52.0	41.0	39.2	38.0	40.6	40.5	42.3	50.9	42.2
All non-work activities	53.1	43.1	43.1	42.9	46.9	47.7	49.1	59.9	47.1
All activities	100.0	100.0	100.0	100.0	100.0	100.0	100.0	100.0	100.0

[1] Housework includes cooking, stamping grain, cleaning, washing, shopping, making or processing goods for own consumption or use, e.g. beer, skins, dresses, pots, etc. (Botswana, 1976, p. 231).

(Table 2, p. 333)

Comments

(a)   "Undoubtedly, people in rural Botswana do not keep
precise track of time during their daily activities; they
merely know that they devoted half of the day to one
activity and half to another.   Therefore the <u>distribution
of time</u> between activities probably is more reliable than
the absolute amount of time spent on activities.   For this
reason the descriptive tables show percentage distributions,
rather than mean amounts of time spent on various
activities" (p. 331).
       "The period not covered by the time use study, February
through April, falls into the busy season.   Thus the time
frame of the study leads to some understatement of economic
activities.   Further, some minor activities seem to be
under-reported in the survey, implying some overstatement of
leisure time.   On the other hand, "rest stops" during
working hours and housework or a leisurely work pace could
lead to a considerable overstatement of working hours"
(p. 331).
       "Opportunities for wage labour are quite limited in
Botswana, particularly for women and children.   ...
Autarchical modes of production imply that asset-poor
households often use family labour to a point where marginal
returns from work are very low ... " (pp. 335-336).

(b)   "Our estimates of the marginal productivity of work
time can only be viewed as approximations since data quality
and statistical procedures are subject to a number of
reservations which have been discussed at some length.   The
robustness of the conclusions nevertheless suggests that our
major findings are valid.   In Botswana the marginal
productivity of work time in rural self-employment is very
low.   People with small holdings of productive assets may
be forced by their poverty to pursue some work which adds
only minimally to income.   They may also slow their work
pace in accord with the available time or in accord with
their nutritional status.   The marginal productivity of
some time inputs by children are close to zero (although
average productivity is no doubt positive).   The
productivity of adult male labour, of women's labour in
female headed households, and of children's labour in cattle
raising households is positive and significant at the
margin, although quite low.   This general result has
important implications for employment policy even if the
calculated regression coefficients and marginal
productivities are not precise" (p. 357).

HENN, 1978

**Peasants, workers and capital: The political economy of labour
and incomes in Cameroon**

Purposes

"An attempt to provide an empirically based <u>and</u>
comprehensive accounting of labour times and related returns (in
cash and subsistence products) of the male head and his wife in
rural Southern Cameroon families" (pp. 162-163).

"To evaluate the effects of price changes on rural welfare
between 1964 and 1974, and to analyse the capacity of various
segments of the wage labour force to reproduce the rural living
standard with wage earnings in 1964 and 1974" (p. 229).

Methods

Data come from a "1964 representative sample survey of rural
labour activities, cash and subsistence returns, and diets
(SEDES, 1966); from three intensive village studies (Guyer,
1978; Wenezoui, forthcoming; Leplaideur; forthcoming) which
cover labour time information over the entire annual agricultural
cycle". These data are supplemented by Henn's own field
observations and from Cameroon's official statistics (labour
force, urban wages, market prices, etc.) (pp. 162-163, 230-231).

(a)   Volume of labour inputs, in time

Time devoted to commodity production, subsistence
production and domestic activities.

(b)   Volume of output, by activity

Weight of firewood gathered and carried home per person
or per worker.

(c) <u>Gross output value, at price
of equivalent market product</u>

"Rural subsistence returns are estimated on the basis
of the physical quantities produced, valued at rural market
prices [i.e.] at the opportunity cost of the physical
product" (p. 166).

(d) <u>Returns in other activities</u>

Domestic production is estimated on the basis of:
number of hours spent in domestic activities
    multiplied by
average hourly return to subsistence plus commodity
production.

(e) The rural standard of living is estimated on the basis
of commodity and subsistence production returns; domestic
production is not included. It corresponds to a
consumption basket which is priced at rural and urban
prices, both for 1964 and for 1974. A comparison with
prevailing wages yields indications on the possibility for
rural and urban wage workers to reproduce the 1964 standard
of living of Southern Cameroonian peasants who farmed their
own land.

"According to a comprehensive 1962-1964 demographic
survey, on average, each active labourer must support at
least one dependent" (pp. 267-268). "If a family of two
adults and two children is to reproduce the rural living
standard in an urban setting, with the wife performing only
domestic labour, the male wage earner or simple commodity
producer must earn twice the amount I call the 'urban cost
of reproducing the rural living standard'" (p. 271).

Results

(a) "The principal male and female adult labourers in the
contemporary peasant families of Southern Cameroon devote
nearly half their combined labour time to subsistence
production, a third to cash-earning activities, and about a
quarter to domestic labour.

On this basis [labour hours], the typical peasant wife
provides a labour contribution to family welfare which is 45
per cent greater than that made by her husband" (p. 167),
i.e. 51 and 35 hours per week respectively in 1964 (table
IV.1, p. 165).

"In 1974, out of the 52 hours of women's weekly labour, 20 were spent on domestic labour" (p. 168).

"The woman's domestic labour consists of over two hours daily in preparing the main evening meal and one half hour warming its leftovers for the next day's breakfast (750 hours per year). Water carrying, clothes and dish washing, and marketing for family consumption needs take up at least 250 more hours per year. Child care is integrated into all other activities. Older children may help with domestic labour but this does not reduce the principal female's labour times below the conservative figures used here" (p. 169).

(b)   "The 440 kilos of firewood per person used to prepare the evening meals each year mean that an average woman carries home at least 2 tons annually" (SEDES, 1966, p. 112, quoted in Henn, 1978, p. 241.)

(e)   In 1964, the yearly commodity and subsistence production returns of peasant families amounted to 90,900 CFA francs for husband and wife together (table IV.1, p. 165), i.e., 45,500 CFA francs per worker or 22,500 CFA francs per person supported.

The small town wage worker was not able to reproduce the 1964 rural standard of living, neither in 1964 nor in 1974. In Yaoundé in 1964, over 30 per cent of the households could not reproduce the 1964 rural standard; by 1974, this proportion had risen to over 60 per cent.

All these results are presented in more detail in the following tables.

(a), (c), (d)

Annual labour hours and cash or subsistence returns: 1964 and 1974

	Women		Men		Total	
	Hours	Return (CFA-fr.)[1]	Hours	Return (CFA-fr.)[1]	Hours	Return (CFA-fr.)[1]
1964						
Commodity production	460	9 500	880	33 000	1 340	42 500
Subsistence production	1 190	29 300	880	19 100	2 070	48 400
Sub-total	1 650	38 800	1 760	52 100	3 410	90 900
Domestic labour	1 000	23 600	60	1 800	1 060	25 400
Total labour	2 650	62 400	1 820	53 900	4 470	116 300
1974						
Commodity production	510	22 500	950	57 500	1 460	80 000
Subsistence production	1 170	60 500	810	34 300	1 980	94 800
Sub-total	1 680	83 000	1 760	91 800	3 440	174 800
Domestic labour	1 000	48 800	60	3 200	1 060	52 000
Total labour	2 680	131 800	1 820	95 000	4 500	226 800
	Percentage distribution of labour time					
Commodity production	19		52		32	
Subsistence production	44		45		44	
Domestic labour	37		3		24	
Total labour	100		100		100	

[1] CFA-francs: US$1.00 = 250 CFA-fr.

(Table IV.1, p. 165)

(a), (c)

Annual labour hours and cash/subsistence returns by category of labour activity, 1964 and 1974 in CFA-francs

	1964			1974		
	Women	Men	Women and men	Women	Men	Women and men

COMMODITY PRODUCTION

	Hours	Return	Hours	Return	Cash income total	Hours	Return	Hours	Return	Cash income total
Cocoa	60	1 400	540	26 400	27 800	60	2 200	540	41 200	43 400
Food crops	250	4 600	30	700	5 200	300	14 600	50	2 600	17 200
Palm wine - men whiskey - women	40	1 300	120	2 400	3 700	40	2 000	120	4 000	6 000
Other commodities	30	600	100	1 900	2 500	30	1 000	150	7 000	8 000
Commerce - women wage work - men	80	1 600	90	1 600	3 200	80	2 700	90	2 700	5 400
Total, commodity production	460	9 500	800	33 000	42 500	510	22 500	950	57 500	80 000

SUBSISTENCE PRODUCTION

	Hours	Market cost[1]	Hours	Market cost[1]	Sub-sistence total[1]	Hours	Market cost	Hours	Market cost	Sub-sistence total[1]
Food crops	970	21 000	190	4 600	25 600	970	46 300	190	10 200	56 500
Meat/fish	90	4 300	160	3 600	7 900	90	5 200	160	8 400	13 600
Palm wine/arki	20	600	330	6 300	6 900	20	1 000	330	10 500	11 500
Firewood	90	2 600	-	-	2 600	90	8 000	-	-	8 000
Household goods and housing	20	800	200	4 600	5 400	-	-	130	5 200	5 200
Total, subsistence production	1 190	29 300	880	19 100	48 400	1 170	60 500	810	34 300	94 800

[1] The opportunity cost of subsistence production was calculated using rural market prices.

(Table IV.2, pp. 170-171)

(e)

Cost of reproducing 1964 peasant standard of living

	1964		1974	
	Rural prices	Yaoundé prices	Rural prices	Yaoundé prices
	CFA-francs			
Total cost per person	22 630	34 315	44 565	66 505
Necessary annual earnings per worker[1]	45 260	68 630	89 130	133 010
Necessary weekly earnings per worker	870	1 320	1 714	2 558

[1] One active worker supporting two persons.

Wages

	1964			1974		
	Rural	Small town	Yaoundé	Rural	Small town	Yaoundé
	CFA-francs					
Minimum wage for a 40 hr week[1]	640	1 160	1 440	1 040	1 600	1 960
Average wage for unskilled worker[2]	750	–	(30% of households below CFA-fr. 1 320)	1 200	–	(60% of households below CFA-fr. 2 558)
Landowning peasant returns for a 30 hour week	870	–	–	1 700	–	–

[1] "Minimum rural wage in capitalist agricultural enterprises; minimum urban wage in industrial and other capitalist or para-public enterprises" (p. 276).

[2] "Unskilled workers, i.e., 90 per cent of the plantation workers in 1964, 93 per cent in 1974" (p. 279).

(Derived from tables IV-1, p. 165 and VI-7, p. 277; also from pp. 276, 279, 282 and 289)

Comments

(a), (c), (d)   "The labour and returns of teenage children and of old persons aged 65 and over are not accounted for" (p. 164).

(c)   The opportunity cost of the physical product is "the amount of cash which would have to be earned in order to replace subsistence production under the economic conditions of the period cited.   No assertion is made that the opportunity costs would remain the same if peasants shifted significantly   away   from   subsistence   and   into commodity-producing activities or vice versa." (Note: The opportunity cost of the physical product should not be confused with the opportunity cost of time used in other evaluations.)

(a), (d)   "There is no really satisfactory way to ascribe a monetary opportunity cost to domestic labour because most domestic services are not sold in rural or urban markets. The consumption of domestic services being considered an essential input into family welfare, an alternative is to simply compare total labour hours using the assumption that all types of labour are equally important" (pp. 166-167).

(a), (c)   "Commodity production has a higher return per labour hour than subsistence production.   Technical and social constraints prevent the wholesale switch from subsistence to commodity-producing   activities   which   these   differing relative returns would theoretically stimulate" (p. 167). "The social relations of patriarchal subsistence still exert a major impact on male and female economic decisions concerning the allocation of their total labour time. Women are constrained by the historically received social definition of their 'obligations' to husband and children - obligations which both make their labour days half again as long as the husband's and restrict the portion they can devote to cash-earning activities to only 19 per cent" (p. 169).   "Both the rising opportunity costs and the crucial importance of women's food producing labour to family welfare have the effect of limiting the rural woman's ability to switch out of subsistence and concentrate her labour on activities which bring the highest cash return. For men, on the other hand, the lesser importance of their subsistence activities allows a great deal of flexibility in the time and effort which can be devoted to alternative cash-earning activities.   These 'constraints' to rational economic choice, and the overburdening of one family economic agent while the other is 'underemployed', are contemporary effects of the patriarchal subsistence social relations of production" (p. 176).
        "Men work only 35 hours a week on all tasks.   Peasant women, in contrast, spend 51 hours a week working.   It is clear that men dispose of sufficient potential labour to

help their wives in food production. The fact that, even with rising returns to commodity food production and falling returns to cocoa, men have not yet shown much of a tendency to work with their wives, speaks to the power of the traditional social relations. These relations are gradually changing, but their remaining influence is still strong. Younger husbands may support their wives' efforts by clearing all their fields and financing their marketing ventures. Men who go further, however, and actually help in the field not only subject themselves to ridicule by the older male villagers, but may be accused of sorcery" (pp. 219-220).

(c)   "Female subsistence labour time has a higher opportunity cost [i.e. return to labour], than male subsistence activities because traditional food products are still the basis of urban diets, but the products of male subsistence labour are either not consumed in town or are replaced with items of foreign or local capitalist manufacture" (p. 175).   "The rapidly rising opportunity cost of food has contradictory effects on the peasant wife. It increases her opportunity to earn a cash income but, at the same time, it does not allow her to reduce labour inputs on the production of food for her family" (p. 257).

(e)   In comparing standards of living, one should keep in mind that wage workers achieve their standard of living by working at least 40 hours weekly while landowning peasants achieve it in 34 hours. It should also be remembered that wage employment in rural areas and rural migration to urban centres are often the lot of younger rural men who are not yet landowners. Their standard of living is lower even in the rural area than that of the landowning peasant. They also tend to have labour obligations towards the elders, which may constitute one more reason for rural youth to seek urban employment.
       "The small town wage worker was not able to reproduce the rural standard as evaluated at Yaoundé prices in either 1964 or 1974. In 1964, however, two factors may have allowed him to live on a par with the rural peasant and the Yaoundé minimum wage worker: food and rent prices in secondary towns are often lower than Yaoundé prices, and, if he were married, the wage worker's wife had a greater opportunity to farm around a small town and could thereby reproduce her normal rural share of the family consumption basket. By 1974, the small town minimum wage worker was much worse off. He could no longer even reproduce 1964 peasant living standards at rural market prices" (p. 281).
"In contrast, only 10 per cent of the women who lived in Yaoundé could find land in order to farm on a full-time basis" (p. 271).

Africa, Cameroon, cont.

In 1964, in Yaoundé, over 30 per cent of the households could not reproduce the rural standard (p. 282). Nevertheless, persons who could find regular wage employment in the private or public sectors could improve upon the typical rural living standard, particularly if part-time artisan and other supplementary labour was available from family members. By 1974, a conservative estimate would place at least 60 per cent of Yaoundé households below 1964 rural living standards (pp. 272, 284, 285 and 289).

Henn's data correspond to gross output value and are therefore not suitable for comparison with wages. Value added would be more suitable, but no figures about monetary inputs into subsistence production, which would enable us to calculate value added, are given in this study.

FEACHEM et al., 1978

Water, health and development

Purposes

To examine village water supplies in the context of rural development and to evaluate any contribution they might make towards this complex social and political process. In particular, if village water supplies are to be seen as a component of successful rural economic development, it is desirable to evaluate them in economic terms (pp. 7-8).

To examine whether, if women could be saved time on a household chore such as water collection, they would spend more time on agriculture, in other words, whether the time-saving benefit from water supplies has an opportunity value to agricultural production (p. 190).

Methods

(a)   Volume of labour inputs, in time

Two sets of data were collected.

Observation of 1,334 household days of water collection and use, from 567 households intensively surveyed in two clusters of villages, one in the lowlands and one in the mountains, confidently taken as representative of the rural economy of Lesotho (p. 90).

The time spent in water collection can be expressed as a percentage of the total available daylight time and energy. These percentages may be calculated for collection of water from the old source and from the improved supply (p. 214).

(b)   Systematic observation of women's activities; compilation of "time budgets" for 57 women at various seasons of the agricultural year (a total of 79 "woman-days") in villages with piped water, in both mountains and lowlands (p. 188).

(c)   Value added, at price of equivalent market product

     If all other benefits (e.g. health) from village water supplies are ignored, the construction of a supply sets an implicit value on women's time, which is calculated as follows:
cost of a typical water supply per adult woman
    divided by
time saved per average adult woman in each of the next ten years "discounted at some suitable rate of interest to the present" (pp. 39 and 191).

Results

(a)   In the following table, the travel time to an improved source is compared to travel time to the spring which was used in the same village before the improved supply was constructed.

Collection times and time savings in villages with and without an improved supply

Mean time (minutes)	Households using springs		Households using taps		Actual reductions	
	Low-lands	Mountains	Low-lands	Mountains	Low-lands	Mountains
Time per journey[1] (round trip)	22	11	8	4	16	8
Time per household per day	99	50	36	18	72	36
Time per person per day	22	11	8	4	16	8
Time spent by adult woman per adult woman per day	41	25	15	9	30	18

[1] These journey times are the round trip travel times with one minute added to allow for collection at a tap and two minutes added to allow for collection at a spring.

(Table 7.6, p. 100)

In a third of the lowland villages, the actual saving per day for adult women has been over one hour. The typical lowlands household using an unimproved supply devotes 99 minutes per day - or 22 minutes per person per day - to water collection. This is only 3 per cent of the available daylight hours (pp. 99 and 100).

(b)   "The amount of time a woman actually spends in water collection will vary ... depending on how many able-bodied females are available to help her with the task.   In fact, the major factor determining how much time a woman is likely to spend on domestic chores in general is the number of women in the household able to help her ... The pattern emerges particularly strikingly in the lowland data ... the more women there are in a household the less each has to spend on household chores ... The time [saved] is almost entirely spent on social and leisure activities, rather than on agricultural work" (p. 190). These results are given in the following table.

Variation in lowland women's time budgets with number of able-bodied women in household

No. of able-bodied women in house-hold	Average time spent per "woman-day" on each activity (minutes)					
	Water collection	Other house-hold work	Agricul-tural work	Social activity etc.	Total	No. of "woman-days" observed
1	33	537	34	238	842	5
2	10	478	70	291	849	14
3	15	375	44	376	810	18
4						
5						
6	7	287	94	524	912	12

(Table 10.3, p. 191)

"We tentatively conclude that the savings in time spent in collecting water, which result from a piped water supply, have only relatively little opportunity value to agricultural production, in the present circumstances of rural Lesotho. However, we do not argue from this finding that the time savings to women who have a piped water supply

are of no value. For many women in Lesotho, domestic life
is arduous and without much comfort, and for them a
reduction in the time that must be spent on one of the most
strenuous of the day's activities is a real benefit and one
that should be recognised as such" (p. 191).

(c)   "This capital cost [incurred in providing a typical
water supply] represents an expenditure of ... approximately
4 cents per hour saved [in the lowlands].   It seems by no
means excessive to value women's time at 4 cents per hour
when much of that time may be spent on miscellaneous, but
necessary domestic duties and child rearing.   Women working
as domestic servants in towns, and doing similar work in
other people's houses are paid around 10 cents per hour"
(pp. 191-192).

Comments

(a)   As points of comparison, "in the New Guinea highlands,
an average of 1.6 per cent of daytime energy is spent in
water collection" (Feachem, 1973b); "in East Africa, a mean
of only 1.8 per cent of the total available energy is spent,
although individual communities can expend up to 4 per cent
and individual households as much as 14 per cent (White et
al., 1972)" (p. 214).
         "The travel times in Lesotho are low when compared to
arid areas or regions having a pronounced dry season.   In
such regions, travel times of well over two hours are not
uncommon.   The volumes of water used [in Lesotho] are large
by African standards" (p. 111).
         "There is evidence that village women set some value on
this saved time.   We found no evidence in Lesotho for the
common supposition that the opportunity for gossip while
waiting for water at the tap has a positive social value"
(p. 187).

(b)   "... agriculture is largely a marginal activity in Lesotho,
and is overshadowed by cash employment in South Africa.
Labour, particularly female labour, is not the main
constraint on agricultural production.   The dominant
constraints are ... cash for seed and fertiliser, land
(particularly for a kitchen garden), and traction for
ploughing" (Murray, 1976) (p. 190).
         "It is clear that the time-budget data which we
collected are not sufficient to allow any definitive
statement concerning the opportunity cost to productive
agriculture of the water collection journey in Lesotho"
(p. 190).

(c)   In this evaluation, the market equivalent of carrying
water is a water supply using purchased equipment.   This
equipment requires only one monetary outlay: the capital

investment. Labour for installing the equipment is supplied on a self-help basis, i.e. not remunerated; its value, which logically ought to be included in the cost of the water supply, would make very little difference to the calculations (Cairncross, Private communication, 1986). There are neither intermediate consumption expenses, nor operating surplus, nor taxes. Value added is therefore equal to capital amortisation which is assumed to occur at a rate of 10 per cent per year.

"... We suggest as an evaluative criterion for water supplies a measure which relates the cost of the scheme to the amount of time which will be saved by the women. This shows the value of women's time implied by a proposed investment in a water supply, which may be used as a means of comparing proposed water supplies that vary in costs and prospective benefits" (p. 195).

"Unskilled labour in Lesotho is paid at a rate of up to 20 cents per hour, but the comparison should not be taken too seriously; cost-effectiveness analysis of this kind is essentially a tool for comparison of alternatives within one sphere of activity, rather than the allocation of resources between sectors of the economy" (p. 215).

The method used here "avoids the invidious task of setting an actual price on time-saving, while allowing comparisons in monetary terms. ... This simple calculation can be carried out on the basis of an estimated cost and a few simple observations" (p. 215).

MURRAY, 1981

Families divided: The impact of migrant labour in Lesotho

Purpose

Theoretical discussion of the contribution of women's unpaid labour to the economics of migration.

Method

"The value of the [migrant's] wife's services was precisely the difference between his putative income as a migrant coal miner and his real income in the informal sector. A man's decision to migrate is conditional on the presence of someone at home who will carry out the essential tasks connected with the rearing of the family" (p. 166).

Result

A case study is given as illustration of this approach.
"Domestic circumstances of household No. 137 in October 1978. M's wife died in December 1977. M. could not undertake a further contract on the Natal coal mine where he was usually employed because there was no one he could trust to look after the four children (aged 8 to 15) properly in his absence from Lesotho. The conventional economic analysis of M.'s decision to migrate or not to migrate proceeds by reference to the marginal product of labour in agriculture. Could he earn more by taking up a mine contract than he could supplement the household's domestic income from agriculture by staying at home? These are not in fact alternatives, since agricultural output partly depends on cash investment from migrant earnings. Even if they were alternatives, however, it can be seen that his dilemma has little to do with choosing between them. It could be argued, rather more plausibly, that the value of his wife's services ... [see Method, above] ... of the family. The only solution was to marry again. He duly did so in April 1979" (p. 166).

Comments

"... inability of neo-classical economics, to impute value
to labour that has no price in the market place. Economic
costs, we are told, have mainly to do with the effects of
migration on agricultural output and with the disutility to
migrants of undertaking employment in a foreign country, far from
home, etc. The precision implied in this exercise is quite
spurious. It wholly fails to take into account that a migrant
makes his decision to migrate not merely with reference to the
differential that he observes between domestically generated
income and his potential earnings as a migrant, but also with
reference to the distribution of labour within the rural
household. ... Women are not mentioned at all; they are neither
conceptualised nor measured" (pp. 165 and 166).

Our interpretation of the example is somewhat different.
It illustrates the fact that M. cannot, with only his work at
home, generate an income equivalent to the total generated by his
work in Natal and by his wife's work at home. On the other
hand, the example illustrates the complementarity of both incomes
(monetary and in kind) in the survival strategy of this and
similar households. Both kinds of incomes are necessary, but
neither per se is sufficient.

PREST and STEWART, 1953

The national income of Nigeria, 1950-51

Purpose

"To produce meaningful and useful national income totals" (p. 1).

Methods

(a)   Bride price

A rough approximation to the value of the "general services" of water-carrying, cooking, cleaning, child-bearing, child-minding and the like may be obtained from sums paid in bride prices to the bride herself, excluding any payments to the bride's parents (pp. 11, 12 and 47).

From direct observation and from published material, a figure of about £10 was retained.

(b)   Value added, at price of equivalent market product

Farm crops are valued in their "most processed" form; for example, cassava has been partly converted to gari, fufu, or "starch" and partly left as fresh tuber. The evaluation is done as follows:

weight of crop, minus a percentage for loss in processing and in storage

multiplied by

retail prices (corresponding provincial retail prices averaged over time and averaged between markets at any one time)

minus

cost of seeds (pp. 26-28).

Firewood consumption, not only that for which licences are granted or that which is sold in the market, but also

including that gathered direct by consumers, is valued as follows:
weight per head (at least 2 lb, "from published and unpublished data, and our own inquiries")
     multiplied by
retail prices (see above) (pp. 31–32).
     "There seems to be no occasion to deduct anything from this figure to arrive at a net value of output as most transport 'expenses' are in respect of headloading or donkeys which are not included elsewhere in our estimates" (p. 32).

Results

(a)   "Our computation of the value of the 'general' intra-household services not already counted elsewhere, is, with great approximation, £4m" (p. 47).

(b)   The values for subsistence agriculture and food processing, or for subsistence firewood are not available separately as, because of the evaluation method, they are included in farm crop production and in total firewood production.
     Using the output approach, the GDP of Nigeria is estimated at:
     £ 597 m (p. 57),
in which farm crops, including elements of local transport and distribution, and the processing of food, amount to
     £ 296 m (p. 47),
and firewood consumption (total value) amounts to not less than
     £ 20 m (p. 31).

Comments

(a)   "It is recognised that this valuation may be controversial and therefore it is shown separately in the main tables. We consider this estimate a mere 'conjecture', with an average standard error of 40 per cent. We are under- rather than over-valuing as we do not count various annual payments (e.g., cloth at the time of Little Salla in the north), nor do we count the functions of husbands and children" (pp. 12 and 111).
     The rationale for adopting the bride price for evaluation purposes is that "it is a payment and not, as often maintained, a pure gift or transfer. If the bride runs away the husband can reclaim the original bride payment or part of it, depending on the length of marriage

and number of children born to him.   Furthermore these
payments are subject to price control" (p. 11).

(b)   "Farm crops are valued in their 'most processed'
form.   To have done otherwise would have meant omitting
from our account an important element of women's activities
properly definable as 'economic'" (p. 26).

"The figures include an element of local transport and
distribution 'output' because valuation is mainly by retail
market prices" (p. 25).

LONGHURST, 1982

Resource allocation and the sexual division of labour: A case study of a Moslem Hausa village in Northern Nigeria

---

Purpose

"To examine the work of women and their access to productive resources, to analyse the determinants of these ... To present empirical material on the returns to work done by women" (pp. 95-6).

Method

Returns in other activities

Data come from field observations of 101 women in a village of the Muslem Hausa in Malumfashi District, in northern Nigeria.

Returns on investment and returns per labour hour in processing food for sale, kuli (fried groundnut presscake) and fura (millet porridge) are calculated (p. 107).

Results

Returns calculated in this study are compared in the table with 1971 and 1972 data for the Zaria area, 60 miles away (Simmons, 1975).

Costs and returns to production of fura and kuli

	Fura					Kuli		
	Malum-fashi	Hanwa[1]		Dan Mahawayi[1]		Malum-fashi	Hanwa and Dan Mahawayi[1]	
	1976	1971	1972	1971	1972	1976	1971-72	1972
Number of observations	12	40	32	16	13	6	72	5
Average amount raw product processed daily (kg)	3.9	8.0	8.1	4.1	5.0	9.8	16.1	15.2
Average daily wages/ profit (N)	0.15	0.30	0.29	0.08	0.15	0.94	0.48	0.11
Estimated hours to produce	5	8	8	5	5	6	6	6
Wages or profit/hour (N)	0.03	0.037	0.036	0.017	0.031	0.157	0.096	0.022
Return on investment (%)	29.1	40.5	35.1	25.8	35.2	18.4	26.6	5.5
Return on investment per hour (%)	5.8	5.0	4.4	5.2	7.1	3.1	5.3	1.1

[1] Simmons 1975, p. 150.

(Table 4.3, p. 108)

As points of comparison, women's hourly wages for working in the fields, in 1976, were as follows, in Naira (N):
N 0.03 for planting crops;
N 0.05 for picking cotton (p. 107).
"Data on returns per hour for male off-farm work are available from an agroeconomic survey carried out in the State of Kano one year prior to this research (Matlon, 1979, pp. 95-6):
N 0.20 for tailoring;
N 0.15 for cap-making;
N 0.13 for selling firewood;
N 0.13 for trading in kola nuts;
N 0.15 for trading in used clothes;
N 0.27 for trading in cloth" (p. 111).

Comments

"It appears that the segregation of tasks is allied not only to the physical separation of the sexes [seclusion] but also to differences in the returns on men's and women's tasks" (p. 111).

"Women prepare food both as a household obligation and as a means of earning cash ... Nearly all midday meals, and a small proportion of evening and morning meals, are purchased" (p. 106).

"The 'industry' which accomplishes this daily food processing task is characterised by its small scale, simple technology and orientation towards its customers. In most cases, the final product is produced from raw materials by only one person, perhaps with the assistance of a young child, using only ordinary household equipment, and it is sold at the place where the customer finds it most convenient to eat" (Simmons, 1975, p. 147, quoted on p. 107).

"A woman's profit per hour from making _fura_ is roughly comparable with what she might get from working in the fields ... _Kuli_ processing requires much higher investment than _fura_ processing (by a factor of ten), and therefore is carried out by the wealthier women" (p. 107).

One of the interesting aspects of these data stems from the fact that they constitute one rare case of market pricing of cooked food, prepared under the same technological circumstances as the food produced for self-consumption in the household.

MACPHERSON and JACKSON, 1975

Village technology for rural development: Agricultural innovation in Tanzania

---

Purpose

To evaluate the comparative costs of intermediate and village technologies, among which are technologies for water supply and for maize shelling. This costing requires a value imputation for unpaid labour.

Method

Value of non-cash benefits

The data come from field observations in a Ujamaa village in the northern part of the United Republic of Tanzania.

Labour is costed at the value of daily keep in the village. "An individual's time even in a partly subsistence society is at least worth, in monetary units, the amount of food he or she consumes" (White, 1972, p. 98, quoted on p. 106).

For an adult working male, the costing was as follows, in Tanzania Shillings (T.Sh.): food, T.Sh.2.16; drink, T.Sh.1.57; cooking expenses, T.Sh.1.00; clothing and household expenses, T.Sh.0.52; total, T.Sh.5.25. "If anything it is an overestimate to avoid the risk of underestimating the 'cost' of village technology" (p. 106).

For women and children, the costing was at 60 per cent of that for men (p. 112).

Results

Water supply

Village technology, using current village skills, is based on implements of even lower cash cost than intermediate technology. In this particular village, 32,000 gallons of water had been supplied annually by women and children carrying 4-gallon tin containers from a stand-pipe situated a mile away. Mechanised technology was introduced in the form of a diesel pump; however, because of water shortage, water was rationed. An alternative (village technology) would have consisted of one ox-cart carrying a 40-gallon drum.

Costs of village water supply

Item	Diesel pump	Ox-cart	Woman-power
Current supply (gallons p.a.)	124 100[1]	37 440	32 434
Initial outlay (T.Sh.)	21 537[2]	2 433	60
Labour cost (T.Sh. p.a.)	3 780[3]	3 276[4]	7 972[5]
Other costs (T.Sh. p.a.)[6]	8 984	457	63
Total annual costs (T.Sh.)	12 764	3 733	8 035
Cost per gallon (cents)	10	10	25

[1] Based on official ration and size of village.
[2] Not including "free" self-help labour.
[3] At government wage rates.
[4] At T.Sh.5.25 per "man-day".
[5] At 60 per cent of T.Sh.5.25 per "man-day" to allow for the fact that labour is supplied by women and children.
[6] Amortisation, interest, repairs and maintenance, fuel.

Source: Authors' field survey.

(Table 6, p. 112)

As a point of reference, "Tanzania per capita income — including subsistence output — in 1971 [was] 657 shillings (East African Statistical Department, Economic and Statistical Review, Nairobi, East African Community, Sep.-Dec. 1972, tables B1 and K1)" (p. 102).

Maize shelling

"Intermediate technology shellers save a substantial amount of labour-time as compared with village technology ones; moreover the work for a whole area can be done on a contract basis by one sheller which is thus worked to full capacity and so covers its costs, while the farmer's needs can be suited by paying either in cash or in kind. This costs less than the maize consumed by domestic labour shelling by hand or village technology" (p. 111).

Comments

"There is, of course, considerable theoretical dispute as to whether such cost [value of daily keep] should be imputed when there is 'surplus labour'; that is when labour time has no alternative productive use" (p. 106).

CAIN, 1977 and 1980

The economic activities of children in a village in Bangladesh

---

Purpose

"To examine the roles of children in the household division of labour in a village in north-central Bangladesh and to attempt to determine their net productivity while living as subordinate members of their parents' household" (pp. 218 and 220).*

Methods

Data come from anthropological field investigations of "120 sets of parents and their children aged 4 and older (a total of 572 individuals), during one year, ... in a village selected as a study site because, in terms of its economy, ecology, population density, and high fertility, it seemed not atypical of the country" (pp. 218-9).

(a)   Volume of labour inputs, in time

"Time budgets were collected every 15 days, for the 24-hour period preceding the interview, each round of data collection lasting for seven days. The data are preliminary. They are taken from the first four rounds and cover only a two-month period (mid-October to mid-December 1976)" (pp. 235-236). (For final time-use results, see Cain et al., 1979.)

(b)   Volume of output, by activity

"In the absence of more precise measures of productivity and labour efficiency of children relative to adults, we use data on

---

* Page numbers refer to the 1980 publication.

wage rates by age to estimate efficiency differences for males ('productivity coefficients')" (pp. 240-1).

Average daily wage for harvest labour by age of worker, for males aged 8-25

Age group	N	Average daily wage (taka)[1]
8-9	4	4.55
10-11	15	5.36
12-13	27	6.32
14-15	50	6.32
16-17	20	6.29
18-19	58	6.65
20-25	96	6.75

[1] The taka value of meals and payment in kind was estimated according to quantities received and the prevailing market price of commodities.

(Table 9.6, p. 241)

"The wage for permanent labour for boys as young as age eight hired on an annual basis by some better-off households to do little else but care for cattle is most often room and board, plus clothes and care in case of illness" (p. 242).
"To illustrate the lower limits of male children's net productivity, some simplifying assumptions are made:
(1) ...
(2) ...
(3) that male children produce that fraction of an adult male's daily output implied by productivity coefficients and productive work-time coefficients (hours worked in productive activity by children as a proportion of hours worked by adults) [derived from work input data, see (a) above]" (p. 243).
The calculation of male children's daily output is then:
daily output by man aged 22-39, expressed in calories
    multiplied by
productivity per unit time coefficient at child's age
    multiplied by
productive time input coefficient at child's age.

Results

(a) The following table summarises the results concerning time budgets.

Average number of hours worked per day by age and sex

Work Activity	Age											
	4-6		7-9		10-12		13-15		16-21		22-59	
	M	F	M	F	M	F	M	F	M	F	M	F
Productive[1]	1.2	0.7	3.5	1.4	6.6	1.3	8.8	2.0	8.8	1.6	8.0	1.8
Housework[2]	0.9	1.2	1.1	3.7	0.6	5.4	0.7	7.0	0.7	7.8	1.1	7.5
Total work	2.1	1.9	4.6	5.1	7.2	6.7	9.5	9.0	9.5	9.4	9.1	9.3

[1] "Labour necessary for generating income and capital. Includes animal care, crop production (including marketing and parboiling paddy), wage work, trading, fishing, and other" (pp. 221; 236-7).

[2] "Labour necessary for the maintenance and upkeep of the household, which is not directly productive in the sense of generating income or contributing to physical capital formation. Includes cleaning and sweeping house and compound, washing clothes and utensils, preparing food (including husking, drying and cleaning of paddy), cooking, providing cooking fuel and water, shopping for home consumption, caring for young children and for other dependents, and countless other small chores" (pp. 221 and 236).

(For detailed breakdown of time inputs, see original publication.)

(Excerpted from table 9.4, p. 237)

(b) "Findings suggest that, in general, male children become net producers at the latest by age 12. When considering only directly productive work, female children do not compensate their total consumption by the time they leave their parents' household" (p. 245). These results are obtained by a calculation illustrated for male children in the next table.

Illustrative calculation of the net productivity of male children

Age group (1)	Average daily per person calorie consumption requirements[a] (2)	Productivity per unit time coefficients[b] (3)	Productive time input coefficients[c] (4)	Average daily product gross[d] (calories) (5)	Average daily product net of consumption[e] (calories) (6)	Exact age (X) (7)	Cumulative productive net of consumption at exact age (X)[f] (calories/365) (8)
1	1 043	0.0	0.0	0.0	− 1 043	1	− 1 043
1–3	1 368	0.0	0.0	0.0	− 1 368	4	− 5 147
4–6	1 368	(0.30)[g]	0.04	59	− 1 309	7	− 9 074
7–9	1 201	0.68	0.23	774	− 427	10	−10 355
10–12	1 728	0.80	0.84	3 327	+ 1 599	13	− 5 558
13–15	2 158	0.94	1.05	4 887	+ 2 729	16	+ 2 629
16–21	2 475.5	1.00	1.11	5 496	+ 3 021	22	+20 755
22–39	2 475.5	1.00	1.00	4 951	+ 2 476	.−	−

a Source: Chen, "An analysis of per capita food grain availability, consumption and requirements in Bangladesh: A systemic approach to food planning", in Bangladesh Development Studies 3, No. 2 (1975): table 5, column e. b Calculated by taking child wage as a proportion of average adult wage. c Calculated by taking child productive work-hours as a proportion of adult productive work-hours for Economic Class III (landless). d Column (3) X Column (4) X 4,951. e Column (5) − Column (2). f Column (6) X person-years in age group indicated in Column (1). g Author's estimate.

Note: For discussion of assumptions, see text.

(Table 9.7, p. 244)

Comments

(a)   "Labour necessary for the maintenance and upkeep of the
household, we characterise as 'enabling' labour in so far as
it frees other household members to engage in activities
that are directly productive.   Many of the activities
characterised as enabling labour could conceivably be
construed as productive.   Husking, for example, adds a
considerable amount of market value to paddy.   Husking is
considered housework in this context, however, because rice
is most often marketed unhusked by cultivators, and husking
at home is practically always for the purpose of home
consumption rather than sale.   These distinctions become
unimportant when one realises the interdependence of
housework and unambiguously productive work.   Both types of
work are 'necessary' and, within limits prescribed by the
nature of social organisations and levels of technology and
affluence, both must to a great extent be satisfied by
household labour" (pp.221-2).

"While it is common in farm accounting to value family
labour at the market price of labour, the opportunity cost
of family farm labour is normally less than the market wage
rate.   The chances of finding employment as a daily wage
labourer are far from certain in this area" (p. 225).

"The [time-input] data are preliminary in two ways:
methodology was evolving and the two-month period, given
great seasonal variations, cannot be taken as representative
of an entire year" (p. 236).

"Class differentials are particularly striking for time
spent in housework.   For example, among adult females those
in large-owner's households do on average two hours more
housework per day than those in landless households.   On
the other hand, with few exceptions, poor females do
considerably more directly productive work than females in
the more well-to-do households.   Neither of these findings
are surprising given that housework requirements increase
with wealth and that poor women have a greater need to seek
wage employment.   Young children among the poor are
delegated household tasks normally performed by older
children or adults in order to permit the latter's
participation in wage employment" (pp. 239-40).

(b)   "Efficiency differences (work output per unit time) by
age for particular activities are related to the age at
entry into the activity.   In general, activities that are
begun at young ages entail small efficiency differences by
age, and a child reaches peak efficiency shortly after he or
she begins.   Among these activities are fishing and
gleaning paddy from fields.   Although it is impossible to
assign a value to efficiency/productivity levels of such
activities, they undoubtedly raise the overall productivity

to some degree. Activities begun at older ages require strength, a higher degree of concentration, and, in some cases, exercise of judgement" (p. 240).

"The imperfection of wage rates as measures of efficiency should be stressed, however. Because employment relations are closely intertwined with a variety of other social relations, both wage rates and access to wage employment vary for a number of reasons other than worker's efficiency" (p. 241).

"If anything the actual returns to a unit of labour, other things being equal, will ordinarily be higher for children who work on land owned by their father than for children who work for a wage. An exception to this is the case of very poor harvests. Under such conditions, hourly or daily wage work can easily be more than hourly or daily returns to family farm labour" (p. 241).

"These calculations are based on preliminary and incomplete data, making a number of assumptions; however, they are quite probably conservative estimates of the net productivity of male children for the majority of households" (p. 243).

"Estimating age differences in efficiency for females is more complicated. Wages cannot be used because the extent of wage employment is much less among females than among males, and the market for their labour is more imperfect with respect to wage determination and access to employment. The impression is that for the majority of activities in which females engage, the efficiency differences by age are not great. Important exceptions are husking and grinding which require considerable strength, and cooking. More important than physical strength, in the general category of food processing and preparation, is the need for skill and judgement in co-ordinating a great variety of different activities. The particular work activities of females are of shorter duration and are more integrally linked than those of males. Thus managerial skills must be applied more frequently, and efficiency is best judged overall rather than for specific activities. For example, in preparing paddy for consumption, a young girl may be as efficient as an adult in mechanically performing a single task, but much less efficient in the complete processing, which requires numerous decisions about quantity and timing. For the most part, women find wage employment in the village in rice processing and as maid servants doing general housework; they are hired to perform a variety of tasks rather than one specific activity, and again managerial skills are at a premium. Because unskilled, inexperienced children require more supervision, few young children engage in this type of wage work. Where young girls work for a wage, they frequently do so in the company of their mother and are normally paid no more than meals for the period of work" (pp. 242-3).

"Although the findings presented above are suggestive, less tentative conclusions regarding the economic roles and contributions of children await further analysis using households rather than individuals as units of analysis. In the context of the rural society of Bangladesh, it is more appropriate to speak of household product than individual product, inasmuch as the activities of individual household members are co-ordinated parts of a single household enterprise" (pp. 246-7).

MUKHERJEE, 1983

Contributions to and use of social product by women

Purpose

"To work out an extended measure of social product including the value of housewives' services ... to chart, with very approximate estimates, large relevant areas in which more refined quantitative estimates can be prepared and deeper analysis can be applied" (pp. 1 and 2).

Method

Returns in other activities

The value of housewives' services is estimated as follows:
number of housewives
    multiplied by
average contribution per worker to the Net Domestic Product (NDP) (pp. 5 and 6).

The number of housewives (i.e. of married women) is estimated from census data at 90 million. Average annual contributions per worker to NDP, taken from computations of the Central Statistical Organisation (India, CSO, 1981), are as follows, in Indian rupees (Rs.):

(a) NDP per worker, in agriculture   Rs. 1,282
(b) NDP per worker, overall national average   Rs. 1,884

Results

Imputed value of housewives' services

(million Rs.)		(percentage of NDP*)
(a)	115,380	33
(b)	169,560	49

*NDP: 345,190

(Based on data from pp. 5-7)

Comments

"An Indian estimate will remain arbitrary and somewhat shaky, particularly in the absence of representative time use data. But it will not be very much inferior to the estimates of some of the flows included in our national income statistics" (p. 4).

"In a proper estimate it is not sufficient if we just add the services of housewives who are not employed; we have to reckon, in addition, these services rendered by employed women and men. In our estimates, we have gone by married women only and hence in concept we have covered the employed women as well. But we have missed girls below 14 or so and men of all ages" (p. 10).

The latter leads to an underestimate which has to be confronted with the potential overestimate resulting from counting all married women as housewives at one work-year per woman, i.e. as full-time housewives whether they are employed or not. Time-use studies generally indicate that employed women devote less time to domestic activities than full-time housewives.

"Economic factors or some conventional social factors enjoin that women are paid less than men even when they do the same job. This social practice affects the housewives' imputed earnings because the evaluation is done at market rates or at opportunity cost based on market rates of earnings of women" (p. 1).

The author uses NDP per worker in different activities (registered manufacturing, unregistered household manufacturing, etc.) in order to indicate possible dimensions of women's contribution when different bases of imputation are used. He concludes that only two methods merit serious attention: overall national average and average in agriculture. While there could be some justification for using the overall average NDP per worker, he does not really recommend this method and finally chooses NDP per worker in agriculture as a preferred method (p. 6 and private communication).

"I think that the average contribution to NDP in agriculture should be a good approximation ... . The Final Report of the National Income Committee shows that the NDP per worker for agriculture was only slightly above that for domestic servants (Rs.472 and Rs.408). However the status of a housewife and the ranges of duties she has to perform are both way above than what we have in mind when we think of a domestic servant, and this is true for poorer strata of the society as well" (p. 6).

HART, 1980

Patterns of household labour allocation in a Javanese village

---

Purpose

Understanding the manner in which rural households allocate their time among income-earning activities, housework, and non-work activities in relation to two broad sets of policy issues: the first, a macro-level focus on the growth potential inherent in the large-scale mobilisation of rural labour; the second a focus on the need to increase directly the welfare of poor households (p. 188).

Methods

Data come from a sample of 87 households stratified on the basis of land ownership, in a village of Central Java (pp. 188 and 194).

(a)   Volume of labour inputs, in time

"The sample households were interviewed every month during the course of a year on the labour allocation of each household member aged six and over, as well as on household income and consumption, during the preceding thirty days. The data presented correspond to two of these monthly interview periods" (p. 199).

(b)   Returns in other activities

Searching activities (fishing, gathering wild vegetables, snails and fuel) are probably valued at market prices.   Although, in this publication, there is no explanation about the evaluation method, indirect evidence points in this direction.   For instance: "Particularly in the wet season, women and children are heavily involved in

gathering vegetables which grow wild in the rice fields;
the vegetables are either consumed at home, sold raw, or
prepared with spices and sold as a cooked dish. All age
and sex groups are actively involved in searching for fuel
for both sale and home consumption; and in certain seasons
snails are plentiful in the rice fields and fetch a high
market price" (p. 196).

Returns to labour per hour are then calculated for wage
labour and searching activities, taking into account
travelling time.

Results

(a) The labour inputs in time, as given in the interviews, are
shown in the first table (Inter-class difference in
household labour allocation ...).

(b) Returns to labour per hour are illustrated in some detail in
the second table (Average hours spent working and returns to
labour ...).

"Women, for transplanting, earned Rp.30 per hour.
Men, for hoeing and removing seedlings from the nurseries,
earned an average of Rp.40 per hour. While the returns to
women and children for gathering vegetables and fuel were in
the vicinity of Rp.11 - Rp.13 per hour" (pp. 199-200).

(a)

Inter-class difference in household labour allocation among income-earning activities and housework

Class averages		Income-earning activities					House-work[d]	Total, income earning and housework
		Own produc-tion[b]	Trading	Wage labour	Searching activi-ties[c]	Total, income-earning activities		
				Hours per month[a]				
Peak month								
Class I[e]	Hours/person[f]	75.9	11.8	17.0	1.8	106.4	42.0	148.4
	% allocation	51.5	7.9	11.4	1.2	71.7	28.3	100
Class II	Hours/person	31.1	12.3	75.7	22.7	141.7	33.9	175.6
	% allocation	17.7	7.0	43.1	12.9	80.7	19.3	100
Class III	Hours/person	6.4	4.0	123.1	19.8	153.3	32.5	185.8
	% allocation	3.4	2.2	66.2	10.6	82.5	17.5	100
Slack month								
Class I	Hours/person	83.9	10.5	6.3	5.6	106.2	44.3	150.5
	% allocation	55.7	7.0	4.2	3.7	70.6	29.4	100
Class II	Hours/person	23.7	16.5	44.8	35.9	120.9	34.3	155.2
	% allocation	15.3	10.6	28.9	23.1	77.9	22.1	100
Class III	Hours/person	9.2	2.8	81.0	62.3	155.4	36.0	191.4
	% allocation	4.8	1.5	42.3	32.5	81.2	18.8	100

[a] Including travelling time. [b] "Own production refers to all work done on production assets 'controlled' (owned or share-cropped) by the household and includes work on rice fields, fish ponds, home gardens, and livestock" (p. 199). [c] Searching activities include fishing, gathering wild food and fuel. [d] "Housework includes processing rice for home consumption, food preparation and fetching water, house cleaning, washing clothes, shopping, and house repair/maintenance. Child-care activities, which are frequently combined with other household tasks, are excluded" (p. 200). [e] Classes are defined according to "control" of rice fields and fish ponds. (Class III includes the poorer households.) [f] Hours per person aged 10 or more.

(Excerpted from table 8.1, p. 202.)

(b)

Average hours spent working and returns to labour per hour at the individual level in wage labour and searching activities

| Age group | Class | Wage labour | | | | Searching activities | | | |
| | | Peak month | | Slack month | | Peak month | | Slack month | |
		Hours	Returns to labour per hour (Rp.)	Hours	Returns to labour per hour (Rp.)	Hours	Returns to labour per hour (Rp.)	Hours	Returns to labour per hour (Rp.)
Females									
6-9	I	0	-	0	-	0	-	0	-
	II	0	-	0	-	0	-	0	-
	III	0	-	0	-	6.8	16.0	2.7	9.0
10-15	I	25.0	20.0	20.0	16.6	0	-	11.7	13.5
	II	34.4	19.5	12.5	13.9	24.7	9.6	7.6	5.6
	III	104.8	20.1	125.4	15.5	2.4	7.3	38.8	11.4
16+	I	24.0	25.9	0	-	3.9	15.3	8.6	11.1
	II	62.9	25.9	29.8	15.9	16.2	16.8	13.9	13.2
	III	89.4	25.2	77.0	15.0	17.9	10.5	23.0	11.2
Average per female 10+	I	24.2	24.5	5.0	16.6	2.9	15.3	9.4	11.9
	II	53.8	24.6	24.2	15.6	18.9	16.8	11.9	14.6
	III	92.6	23.9	86.5	15.2	16.0	10.5	26.6	11.2
Males									
6-9	I	0	-	0	-	0	-	0	-
	II	0	-	0	-	0	-	0	-
	III	8-4	10.9	0	-	0	-	4.6	14.6
10-15	I	0	-	0	-	1.6	14.3	6.9	11.5
	II	23.4	28.8	5.0	5.0	42.3	15.5	61.0	18.7
	III	36.4	31.3	8.4	21.4	41.9	19.6	97.4	14.6
16+	I	15.9	38.2	10.5	47.6	0.4	25.0	0.4	23.1
	II	129.5	37.4	91.0	39.5	18.0	19.2	54.6	42.5
	III	214.3	30.6	104.6	32.5	14.7	22.6	103.8	34.8
Average per male 10+	I	10.7	38.2	7.3	47.6	3.3	18.2	2.4	12.7
	II	94.7	36.7	62.8	38.6	25.9	17.2	56.7	34.1
	III	156.5	30.3	75.4	30.6	23.9	20.8	103.2	27.9

(Table 8.5, p. 210)

Comments

"Particularly in the poorer households, children in the 6-9 age group perform a considerable proportion of child-care duties. Inter-class differences in child-care patterns are reflected in considerably lower school attendance rates for children in the landless households" (p. 200).

(a)   "There are marked qualitative differences in the types of income-earning activities undertaken by households in Classes I and III; in Class III households, income-earning activities are concentrated in heavy manual labour, whereas much of the work done in Class I households involves supervision of hired labourers" (p. 201).

"The table reveals noticeable inter-class differences in the absolute and proportionate amount of time spent in income-earning activities and household work. The average person aged ten or more in a landless household spent about 154 hours per month in income-earning activities (own production as well as other forms of self-employment and wage labour) in both the peak and slack months as opposed to 106 hours per person in a relatively large landowning household" (p. 201).

"The converse of this is a strong relationship between class status and the absolute and proportionate amount of time spent by women in housework. Class I housholds spend between 50 and 60 more hours per month in housework than Class III. These differences are even more significant if account is taken of inter-class variations in household technology. For food preparation, the type of stoves and the cooking utensils used by Class I households are generally more efficient than those used in poorer households. The comparatively high duration of food preparation in Class I households is attributable both to greater frequency and more elaborate types of food prepared. A second major source of inter-class disparities in time spent in housework derives from patterns of shopping. Class I households generally do most of their shopping in the local town where food prices are lower and the range of goods available is more extensive than in the village; wealthier women often spend nearly the whole morning shopping once or twice a week. Class III households, in contrast, do most of their shopping on a day-to-day basis from nearby shops in the village; shopping is usually done in the late afternoon when women return from work, and takes no more than a few minutes. While all households sweep and clean every day, there is a very strong direct relationship between asset status and house size, number of rooms, and the amount of furniture. In general, therefore, goods and time tend not to be substitutable; on the contrary, increases in household capital are complemented by a rise in the absolute and proportionate amount of labour-time spent in housework, and this additional time probably contributes substantially to household welfare" (p. 203).

EVERS, 1981

The contribution of urban subsistence production to incomes in Jakarta (1981a)

Subsistence production and wage labour in Jakarta (1981b)

Purpose

    The main purpose of the survey was to determine what Jakarta's low-income population regard as their own basic needs and how far they are being satisfied. Special attention is given to the contribution of goods and services provided by the consumers themselves (1981a, pp. 89 and 92).

Method

Gross output value, at price
of equivalent market product

    The data come from a random sample of 1,083 households in three selected areas of East Jakarta, interviewed between June and August 1979. "They were divided into ten subsamples, each using a questionnaire with a common part and a special schedule focusing on one particular 'basic need'" (1981a, pp. 91-92).
    "Subsistence production includes agricultural production [for own consumption] still carried on even in the completely urbanised areas of Jakarta, in small house plots, in vegetable gardens along canals, railway lines and roads ... chickens, ducks and other animals are kept, construction and maintenance of houses, collection of firewood and water, processing of food, sewing of own clothes, health care, recreation and transport" (1981a, p. 93) and "food transfers from the rural subsistence sector" (1981b, p. 20).
    "Subsistence goods and services are calculated at current local market prices" (1981a, p. 94).

Results

"According to our survey data, subsistence production contributed about 18 per cent to the total consumption expenditures of households in East Jakarta.

According to one of our subsamples of 120 households, 16.7 per cent of food derived from subsistence production.

More relevant is the strategic importance of subsistence production for low-income households. For about one-third of the survey households, subsistence production contributed more than 20 per cent of monthly household expenditure" (1981a, p. 94). These results are shown in the two following tables.

However, "among these subsistence producers, poor households are over-represented. In fact, the subsistence production index (measuring subsistence production as a percentage of total household consumption) correlated negatively with monthly household money expenditures (r = -0.38)" (1981a, p. 94).

"Half the workers [in the informal sector] had to add more than 30 per cent in terms of subsistence production to their incomes in order to survive ... subsistence production is subsidising wage labour, and, in fact, enables the payment of wages below the subsistence level and the poverty line" (1981b, p. 25).

Subsistence production as a percentage of total household consumption

Households		Subsistence production as a percentage of total consumption
No.	%	
54	5.0	0
231	21.3	0.1-10
435	40.2	10.1-20
220	20.3	20.1-30
143	13.2	30+
1 083	100.0	
		Mean = 18 per cent

(1981a, table 3, p. 95)

Average subsistence production by income groups

Household income in Rp.1,000	Averages			Number of households
	Household income (Rp.)	Subsistence production (Rp.)	Subsistence production index[1] (%)	
0- 10	8 750	1 800	16.73	8
11- 20	16 220	4 270	22.59	45
21- 30	26 660	6 660	22.49	105
31- 40	35 650	7 070	19.44	166
41- 50	45 810	8 430	18.31	180
51- 60	55 510	9 590	16.99	178
61- 70	65 080	9 350	15.10	120
71- 80	75 890	13 180	17.35	74
81- 90	85 580	10 850	13.53	70
91-100	95 050	14 860	16.17	44
101-110	104 690	15 310	15.61	29
111-120	115 120	14 290	11.65	18
121-130	125 480	11 670	11.09	16
131-140	139 000	11 000	10.95	3
141-150	147 310	22 150	15.56	10
150 and above	190 930	11 710	7.67	17
Total	58 630	9 380	17.56	1 083

Correlation average household income/subsistence production index: r = -0.8504

[1] Subsistence production at market prices as percentage of total household expenditure.

(1981b, table 9, p. 23)

Comments

"The sample of 1,083 households which forms the basis of the analysis is not representative of the Jakarta population in a statistical sense, though the distribution of a number of important parameters resembles those of the total Jakarta population.   But it can be regarded as fairly 'typical' of the kampong dwellers of the Indonesian capital, who account for some 80 per cent of total Jakarta population" (1981a, p. 92).

"Coverage of all subsistence goods and services was by no means complete.   Valuation of subsistence production, particularly of services, presents special problems since the products and services derived from the subsistence production sector are not sold on the market.   We have attempted to estimate current local market prices for services and goods consumed.   Some sociologists would argue that subsistence production is not directly determined by market forces but by social demand for the satisfaction of basic needs (Elwert and Wong, 1980)" (1981a, p. 94).

"Although our data are still inadequate and prone to sampling and other errors, they at least point to the importance of subsistence production as a third sector in the urban economy next to the formal and the recently 'discovered' informal sector producing for the market.   The maintenance of subsistence production may, indeed, be of strategic importance for the satisfaction of basic needs and the survival of low income groups in a metropolitan environment" (1981a, pp. 95-96).

"Our original hypothesis that subsistence labour becomes relatively more important with declining household income was only partly confirmed.   In fact for the very poor households, subsistence labour, though still essential for their survival, amounted to a lesser share than for somewhat 'richer' households.   Access to land and resources, 'capital equipment' for household production, like sewing machines, a stove, or a bicycle, appear to be as important as the composition of the household labour force or the dependency ratio [i.e., the proportion of children (aged less than 14) plus old people (aged 66 and above) to adult household members (aged 15-65).   (Evers, Pitomo et al., 1982, p. 36)].   For similar reasons the total value of subsistence income increases with growing household income, while its relative value declines" (Evers, 1984, pp. 12-13).

INDONESIA and NEPAL
1972-73
rural

NAG, WHITE and PEET, 1978 and 1980

An anthropological approach to the study of the economic value
of children in Java and Nepal

Purpose

"To assess and compare the actual economic value of children
to their parents in two peasant communities, one in Java and one
in Nepal" (p. 249).*

Methods

Data come from anthropological field investigations of
relatively isolated villages, and include 20 Javanese medium- and
low-income households and about 50 (106 for part of the year)
Nepalese intermediate caste (Thami) households, observed during
18 to 22 months.

(a)   Volume of labour inputs in time

"In the Javanese village, time-allocation data on household
members for a particular day were collected mainly by
interviewing the household members on the following day,
although these were checked and supplemented by occasional
observations.   In the Nepalese village, these data were
collected mainly through observation and supplemented by
occasional interviews" (p. 268).

---

* Page numbers refer to the 1980 publication.

(b)   <u>Returns in other activities</u>

Throughout the year, data were also collected, in the
Javanese households, on income and expenditure.   With these
data, it was possible to estimate the returns per hour of
labour in different occupations (i.e. market-oriented
activities), at prevailing prices and wages.   For instance,
the returns per hour of labour were estimated for
"preparation of food for sale", a market-oriented activity
very similar to the subsistence activity "household food
preparation".

Results

(a)

Average time input (in hours) per day in different work activities among various age groups

Males, Javanese village	Age group and sample size							
Activity	6-8 (6)	9-11 (7)	12-14 (10)	15-19 (6)	20-29 (5)	30-39 (9)	40-49 (8)	50+ (3)
Household maintenance[a]	1.9	1.4	1.5	0.3	0.4	1.5	0.5	0.3
Directly productive[b]	1.7	1.7	3.2	7.6	8.3	7.9	8.2	7.0
Total, all work	3.6	3.1	4.7	7.9	8.7	9.4	8.7	7.3

Females, Javanese village	Age group and sample size							
Activity	6-8 (7)	9-11 (4)	12-14 (6)	15-19 (5)	20-29 (9)	30-39 (11)	40-49 (4)	50+ (4)
Household maintenance[a]	2.3	2.4	4.0	3.7	4.9	6.7	4.5	3.8
Directly productive[b]	1.2	3.0	4.7	6.5	7.1	5.2	6.0	4.6
Total, all work	3.5	5.4	8.7	10.2	12.0	11.9	10.5	8.4

Males, Nepalese village	Age group and sample size							
Activity	6-8 (23)	9-11 (31)	12-14 (51)	15-19 (29)	20-29 (20)	30-39 (22)	40-49 (33)	50+ (31)
Household maintenance[a]	0.7	1.7	1.8	2.0	1.6	2.5	2.5	1.9
Directly productive[b]	3.0	4.8	5.5	7.5	8.8	8.7	7.9	7.4
Total, all work	3.7	6.5	7.3	9.5	10.4	11.2	10.4	9.3

Females, Nepalese village	Age group and sample size							
Activity	6-8 (29)	9-11 (30)	12-14 (25)	15-19 (33)	20-29 (28)	30-39 (50)	40-49 (34)	50+ (26)
Household maintenance[a]	2.4	2.6	3.3	3.2	3.7	6.9	5.6	4.4
Directly productive[b]	2.5	5.8	6.6	8.1	8.4	7.2	7.1	6.3
Total, all work	4.9	8.4	9.9	11.3	12.1	14.1	12.7	10.7

[a] Includes child care, household food preparation, firewood collection and other household maintenance work. [b] Includes animal care, wage labour, handicrafts, reciprocal labour exchange, irrigated rice cultivation (own land), garden cultivation (own land), trading, preparation of food for sale, etc. (For detailed breakdown of time inputs, see original publication.)

(Excerpted from tables 10.1, 10.2, 10.3 and 10.4 and from pp. 251-254)

(b)

Returns to labour, per hour, in various market-oriented
activities (rupiahs)

Javanese village	Rp./hr.
Rice cultivation	
Owner-cultivator (0.5 ha)	50
Owner-cultivator (0.2 ha)	25
Share-cropper (0.2 ha)	12.5
Garden cultivation	25
Agricultural wage labour	
Plough (own animals)	70-90
Hoe	9-11
Transplant	6-7
Weed	9-11
Harvest	16-20
Non-agricultural wage labour	
Carrying/construction	10
Crafts (carpentry)	15
Weaving	7
Trade	
Women on foot, Rp.1,000 capital	5-10
Men on foot, Rp.1,000 capital	15
On bicycle, Rp.15,000 capital	20
Preparation of food for sale	
Coconut sugar (own trees)	5-6
Coconut sugar "share-cropping"	2.5-3
Fried cassava	3.5
Fermented soybeans	5
Animal husbandry	
Ducks	5-12
Goats	1-2
Cattle	4-6
Goat and cattle "share-cropping"	2-3
Handicrafts	
Pandanus-leaf mats	1.5
Bamboo mats	3

(Excerpted from table 10.9, p. 261.)

Comments

(a)   "The two field situations required the adoption of different methods for collection of time-allocation data. Hence the use of these data for absolute comparisons between the two villages is somewhat questionable; however, comparisons within each village (e.g., between age-sex groups) may be made with greater confidence" (p. 269).

"The daily average number of hours spent in a specific activity should not be taken to mean that the activity is performed more or less every day throughout the year, and a daily average figure of 0.0 hour for an activity does not necessarily mean that it is never performed by any member of the age-sex group in question" (p. 250).

"The abbreviations 'household maintenance' and 'directly productive' are not intended to suggest that the former are in any way less productive than the latter.   A large part of 'household maintenance' represents a 'prior demand' on the household's time which is no less a logico-physical prerequisite of household consumption and/or survival than wage labour, cultivation, and so on; time must be allotted to these activities before the household can consider engaging in activities directly productive of cash or physical produce (p. 282).   ... The smallest households devoted up to 52 per cent of their total working time to household maintenance tasks and thus had little time left in which to obtain income, while the larger labour units were able to spend up to 81 per cent of their working time directly in the acquisition of income" (p. 284).

(b)   "The term 'returns per hour of labour', rather than the perhaps more convenient 'labour productivity', has been used because the emphasis is on the returns accruing to the producer from a given amount of work, rather than on the quantity of goods produced by that work (or its market value).   The difference in values can be considerable in work whose product does not belong to the worker (e.g., in wage labour, share-cropping, etc.)" (p. 262).

"Our data do not permit precise calculation of the net economic value of children ... [i.e.,] the total discounted flow of direct and indirect future benefits after subtracting the total flow of direct and indirect future costs" (p. 285).

(a), (b) "In contrast to the generally accepted view that rural unemployment and underemployment are widespread in densely populated Java, ... the adult men (15 years or older) in these households expended on the average almost eight hours daily, and adult women almost six hours daily, in directly productive work.   When child care, food preparation, and the various other necessary tasks of household maintenance are included, average inputs of all work rise to 8.7 hours

per day for men and 11.1 hours per day for women.   It is
erroneous to categorise the people doing so much work as
unemployed or underemployed, even though the economic
returns from many occupations are indeed quite low" (p. 262).

"Although agricultural labour brings the greatest
economic return, the major portion of the working time of
most people is spent in non-agricultural activities in which
the return per hour is relatively low.   At least in these
Javanese and Nepalese villages, there is no unemployment or
underemployment, although there is underproductivity per
unit of labour time.   The problem of underproductivity in
these villages makes it essential for children and adults to
spend long hours in both directly productive and
household-maintenance work.   The failure to recognise the
multiplicity of occupation in peasant societies may be a
reflection of the Western stereotype that each person
normally has one 'job' or means of livelihood" (p. 268).

LORFING AND KHALAF, 1985

The economic contribution of women and its effect on the
dynamics of the family in two Lebanese villages

Purpose

"To assess the economic contribution of women aged 15 and
above in terms of both earned and imputed incomes, to identify
the basic determinants of this contribution and its impact on
family dynamics and on women's status" (p. 2).

Methods

The data come from market surveys (wages, prices, etc.) and
from in-depth interviewing of a purposive sample of 51 households
illustrating a variety of socio-cultural backgrounds in two
villages in the Beqaa region (pp. 5 and 9).

(a)   Wage, substitute agricultural worker

The value of work in the fields as unpaid family workers is
imputed from
number of days spent by women in agricultural work
        multiplied by
wages paid to women in this sector and area for different
tasks (p. 9).

(b)   Value added, at price of equivalent market product

The value of goods produced by women is computed from
quantities consumed by the household
        multiplied by
prices of agricultural products and of processed and
preserved food items of different quality brackets
        minus

costs of inputs required for the production of these commodities (seeds, fertilisers, rental rates for land, use of agricultural equipment and transport, etc.) (p. 10).

Results

(a), (b) In the 51 households under consideration "imputed income generated by women through work in the fields and the production of agricultural produce, processed and preserved food items and dairy products that are domestically consumed" (p. 10) is shown below:

Imputed income generated by women

No. of households	% of total household income[1]
12	1-5
13	6-10
9	11-15
4	16-20
3	21-25
5	26-30
5	31-35

[1] "Net earned income and net imputed income generated by all household members during a year" (p. 7).

(Excerpted from table 5, p. 19)

Comments

"Daily housekeeping, cooking and child rearing that are part of domestic production are excluded because of difficulties in quantifying and monetising them. The non-availability of labour substitutes for such chores in the area made any attempt at their monetisation highly inaccurate" (p. 7).

"Given the small size of the sample and the wide diversity prevailing in the Lebanese rural areas, the results of this study cannot be used as a basis for generalisations and specific policy recommendations at the national level. Furthermore, the definition of women's productivity, the quantification of the economic contribution of women, as well as that of the total household income, ought to be considered, at best, as orders of magnitude. The figures quoted are based on certain assumptions.

Changing these assumptions would obviously alter the results" (p. 3).

"Women found it difficult to provide us with a precise time budget for each activity because these activities are often performed simultaneously and/or collectively by all women in the household along with relatives and neighbours. But, in most cases, they could recall quite accurately the amounts of output generated, particularly in the case of food preservation and processing and the number of workdays in agriculture" (p. 8).

KUSNIC and DA VANZO, 1980

Income inequality and the definition of income: The case of Malaysia

---

Purpose

To examine the distribution of four measures of household income of increasing comprehensiveness, and of three alternative measures accounting for variations in the number of hours worked.

Methods

Data are derived from a random sample of 1,064 households in Peninsular Malaysia with at least one ever-married woman less than 50 years of age, interviewed three times at four-monthly intervals (Malaysian Family Life Survey, primarily designed to study fertility and closely related topics.) Only household members aged 15 or older are accounted for (pp. 2 and 13).

Four measures of household income are considered:

Market income which includes wages, net business income, and capital and interest income; it is calculated as the sum of the household's monetary receipts derived from formal market transactions in these three areas.

Total observable income which includes in-kind income, transfer income, value of housing services, and cottage industry income, in addition to market income.

Total actual income I includes the value of housework (cleaning house, washing clothes, shopping and other tasks), in addition to total observable income.

Total actual income II includes the value of cooking and caring for own children, in addition to total actual income I (p. 14 and table 1, p. 16.).

Three additional income measures "do not differentiate between leisure time and non-market work time as do the four above measures.   These new income composites are denoted as:

Standardised observable income.
Standardised actual income I.
Standardised actual income II.

These measures adjust for the variation in hours of work (and hence hours of leisure consumption) implicit in each of the unstandardised income measures by evaluating the corresponding income measure at a common number of hours for all adults in the sample. The common measure is the mean or the number of hours sample members spent performing those activities encompassed in the corresponding unstandardized measure" (p. 15). "That is, we add or subtract from each adult's income an estimate of the value of leisure consumed or forgone in the process of achieving the income we previously attributed to him" (pp. 19-20).

Gross output value, at price of equivalent market product and opportunity cost of time

In-kind income includes, among others, in-kind benefits received in wage-paying jobs, and home-consumed products of the family farm or business. Its gross output value is obtained as follows:
quantities reported
     multiplied by
own-sales prices. (Where the household sold none of the products, sample mean sales prices are used) (p. 18).
Cottage industry income is closely related to in-kind income. It includes goods and services produced and consumed by the household, for which neither a physical description nor an estimate of their value was provided in the survey. Its value, as well as the value of housework and of cooking and child care are obtained by the opportunity cost of time method, as follows:
number of hours reported in the activity by each household member
     multiplied by
his/her wage rate (for individuals without an observed wage, the predicted value generated by a wage regression is used)
     summed up
across all adults in the household (pp. 14; 18-19).

Results

The four measures of household income are shown in the following table in order of increasing comprehensiveness.

Components of income and alternative definitions of household
income

Income component	Mean level (M$/year)	%
Wage income	4 986	39.0
Business income	2 830	22.1
Capital and interest income	403	3.2
	8 219	64.3
Market income	8 219	64.3
Transfer income	131	1
Value of housing services	352	2.8
In-kind income	416	3.3
Cottage industry income	499	3.9
	1 398	11.0
Total observable income	9 617	75.3
Value of housework	1 410	11.0
Total actual income I	11 027	86.3
Value of cooking and child care	1 754	13.7
Total actual income II	12 781	100.0

(Table 2 and fig. 1, p. 22)

"Thus the broadest measure of household income has a mean 56
per cent higher than the narrowest measure; median household
total actual income II is over twice the size of median household
market income; and the household total actual income II of the
poorest decile of the population is over 3.6 times the
corresponding figure for market income. Indeed, broadening the
definition has the greatest impact on the poorest segments of the
population. When the definition of income is broadened from
market income to total income II, the income share of the poorest
20 per cent of the population more than doubles.
When we standardise the income measures, the income share of
the poor is smaller for each standardised income measure than for
the corresponding unstandardised measure, particularly under the
broadest definition of income. This suggests that failure to
adjust for leisure consumption results in an overstatement of the
relative income position of the poor. The poor in Malaysia

appear to attempt to compensate for their relatively low market
income by producing many goods and services for their own
consumption ... But the poor tend to work relatively long hours
at these household production activities and hence forgo
relatively large amounts of potential leisure consumption.
Ignoring this implicit cost of household production tends to bias
estimates of the relative welfare position of the poor upward.
Standardising for leisure consumption causes considerable changes
in households' rankings in the income distribution" (pp. v-vi).

"Our results show that conclusions about the extent of
income inequality within Peninsular Malaysia or among its ethnic
subgroups are very sensitive to how broadly income is defined as
well as to the other factors examined. As an illustration, one
measure - mean household market income - yields a conclusion that
Chinese income is 177 per cent higher than Malay income, while
another very plausible measure - median urban per adult total
actual income II - reduces this number to only 17 per cent"
(p. viii).

Comments

(b)   "We have separated cooking meals and caring for
children from other types of household work for several
reasons:
1.   potential measurement error for there is considerable
     ambiguity in the precise definition of these activities;
2.   perhaps more than other household activities, cooking
     and child care may be done jointly with other
     activities;
3.   the question of whether cooking and child care are
     purely productive activities or joint productive
     activities" (pp. 14-15).

"Due to the obvious problems involved in determining
the actual number of hours one spends in cooking meals or
caring for children, we advise caution in the interpretation
of results relating to the income composite generated by
inclusion of this component" (p. 19).

"Opportunity cost is a lower-bound estimate of the
value of time spent in non-market activities" (p. 4).

"The sample is not representative of the entire
population of Peninsular Malaysia, and our estimates of
levels and inequality of income should be interpreted with
care. None the less, we feel that this sample (which
represents around three-quarters of the population of
Peninsular Malaysia) can still provide useful information on
what happens to the distribution of income when the
definition of income is broadened" (p. 2).

NAG, WHITE and PEET, 1978 and 1980

An anthropological approach to the study of the economic
value of children in Java and Nepal

The data relative to Nepal in this study are discussed above
under Asia, INDONESIA and NEPAL, 1972-73.

Asia
NEPAL
1980
rural

ACHARYA and BENNETT, 1981 and 1983

The rural women of Nepal: An aggregate analysis and summary of eight village studies (1981)

Women and the subsistence sector: Economic participation and household decision making in Nepal (1983)

Purpose

"In the context of the broader issue of women's status, to investigate the relationship between the extent and the structure of women's economic participation and their relative input into household economic decisions ... focus on the subsistence sector and its interaction with the market sector in traditional economies" (1983, pp. i and vii).

Methods

Data come from a "comprehensive micro-level data set collected in eight purposively selected villages to encompass as much as possible of Nepal's wide ethnic and geographic variation. The households (35 in each village, covering between 20 and 100 per cent of the villages' total population) were selected to reflect the villages' caste composition" (1981, p. 10).

Quantitative survey-type questionnaires were combined with in-depth anthropological approaches such as participant observation, open-ended key-informant interviews and, most importantly, extended residence in the community under study" (1983, pp. 1, 4 and 18).

(a)   Volume of labour inputs, in time

Time-use recorded by field observers for all members of 24 households in each village; each day, two spot checks at randomly chosen hours of two groups of six households, between 4 a.m. and 8 p.m.; over six months to a year, i.e. between 78 and 156 observations per household (1983, pp. 7, 64 and 65).

(b)   Value added at price of equivalent market product

For animal husbandry, poultry, agriculture (including kitchen gardening), hunting and gathering, fetching and preparing fuel, manufacturing (including sewing) and food processing (1983, pp. 69-70), value added is derived from:
quantities of goods produced
    multiplied by
market price
    minus
transportation costs, value of raw materials (bought and home produced) and interest charges   (Status of Women Project Team: Field manual ..., 1979, Appendix VI, forms 70 to 72).

For example in the valuation of food processing done at home, "since much of the food processing involved home-produced raw materials, the following procedure was adopted: the market cost of raw materials, e.g. paddy and cash and kind cost involved in processing (milling charges if any) were deducted from the total market value of the processed good (husked rice in this case) and the difference taken as the income generated by food processing within the household" (1981, p. 15).

(c)   Wage, substitute household worker, specialised

For construction, i.e. building and repairing house (living quarters), compound or field fences, animal sheds, well-digging, etc., the following procedure is used:
time inputs
    multiplied by
local market wage rate at the season in which the activity was carried out (1983, pp. 70-71 and Status of Women Project Team: Field manual ..., 1979, Appendix III, p. 2).

(b) and (c) To allocate the imputed income to different sex/age groups, it was distributed between household members on the basis of the proportion of time spent in the various types of activities (1981. p. 166).   "For example, to derive the percentage contributed by men and women respectively to each separate category of household production, factor this production by the amount of time spent in that category of activity by adult males and females of the household" (Status of Women Project Team: Field manual ..., 1979, Appendix III, p. 3).

Results

(a)

Time use pattern by sex, for population 15 years and above (six villages)

(in hours per day)

	Male	Female	Both
I. Work burden			
1. Conventional economic activities			
Animal husbandry	1.43	0.97	1.17
Agriculture	2.73	2.74	2.73
Manufacturing	0.42	0.45	0.44
Outside income-earning activities (in village)	1.24	0.46	0.81
Subtotal for conventional economic activities	5.81	4.62	5.15
2. Expanded economic activities			
Hunting and gathering	0.17	0.05	0.11[a]
Fuel collection	0.24	0.38	0.32[b]
Water collection	0.07	0.67	0.40
Household construction	0.25	0.08	0.16
Food processing	0.18	0.97	0.62
Subtotal for expanded economic activities	0.91	2.16	1.60
3. Domestic activities			
Cooking/serving	0.27	2.05[c]	1.25
Washing dishes	0.03	0.39	0.23
Cleaning house	0.04	0.46	0.27
Laundry	0.02	0.15	0.09
Shopping	0.24	0.17	0.20
Other domestic	0.04	0.13	0.09
Child care	0.16	0.69	0.45
Subtotal for domestic activities	0.79	4.03	2.57
Subtotal for work burden (1+2+3)	7.51	10.81	9.32
II. Maintenance and leisure			
4. Education	0.43	0.10	0.25
5. Personal maintenance	1.45	1.12	1.27
6. Social activities	0.31	0.16	0.23
7. Leisure	6.30	3.81	4.93
Subtotal for maintenance/leisure (4+5+6+7)	8.49	5.19	6.68
III. Total in-village activities	16.00	16.00	16.00

[a], [b], [c] On the original table, these figures read respectively 0.32, 0.11, 0.05; they, however, do not match the other figures and are probably typing mistakes.

(1981, table 3.1, p. 158)

<u>(b),(c)</u> For the 280 households under consideration (1981, table 2.7, p. 36):
- 81.4 per cent of household income is generated in the household, of which:

48.4	farm production
2.6	kitchen gardening
8.1	animal husbandry
4.8	hunting and gathering (including fuel)
1.9	manufacturing
15.6	food processing;

- 18.6 per cent of household income is generated outside the household, of which:

11.7	wages, salaries
6.9	investments, trade;

14.8 per cent of household production is sold, i.e. 12 per cent of household income is derived from goods produced in the household and sold in the market (p. 35). Thus:
- 69.4 per cent of household income is subsistence income (exclusive of domestic activities and of water fetching);
- 30.6 per cent is income generated with market intervention.

The subsistence and non-subsistence origin of income does not differ much between the three economic strata adopted for this study (1981, table 2.10, p. 40). Villages, however, do display significant differences in the proportion of income which is generated through market intervention: subsistence production accounts for 51.7-82.4 per cent of household income depending on the village (1981, table 2.11, p. 41).

With regard to household income:
- 49.80 per cent is contributed by adult women, 44.60 per cent by adult men and 5.60 per cent by children.

   The breakdown of contributions to household income by activity, sex and age are shown in the following table.

Contributions to household income by activity, sex and age[1]

Activities	Adults 15+		Children 10-14		Total
	Male	Female	Male	Female	
1. Animal husbandry	69 115 (46.95)	50 069 (34.01)	12 440 (8.45)	15 590 (10.59)	147 218 (100)
2. Agriculture	45 827 (45.79)	49 019 (48.98)	18 615 (1.86)	33 728 (3.37)	100 081 (100)
3. Hunting and gathering	40 589 (43.70)	45 289 (48.76)	1 793 (1.93)	5 211 (5.61)	92 882 (100)
4. Manufacturing	15 698 (43.05)	19 899 (54.57)	332 (0.91)	536 (1.47)	36 465 (100)
5. Food processing	30 054 (10.75)	236 878 (84.73)	2 544 (0.91)	10 092 (3.61)	279 568 (100)
6. Profit from trading	58 220 (60.33)	38 283 (39.67)	-	-	96 503 (100)
7. Wage and salary	154 902 [77.01]	42 932 [21.34]	1 385 [0.69]	1 925 [0.96]	201 144 [100]
Total household income	826 853 [44.60]	923 547 [49.80]	37 109 [2.00]	67 082 [3.60]	1 854 591 [100]

[1] Income figures are in Nepalese rupees (NR). The figures in parentheses are percentages of total work time. The figures in brackets are percentages of total income.

Note: These estimates have two components, namely, the wage and salary income and all other income. Classification of wage, salary and pensions by age and sex groups presented no difficulty, since the individual contributors could be identified easily. Income generated in other sectors have been allocated to different age/sex groups in proportion to the time spent by these age/sex groups in respective sectors. For example, in the 167 sample households a total income of NR147,218 was generated from the activities classified under animal husbandry. Since adult female time constituted 34.01 per cent of the total time spent by all members of the same sample households on these activities, 34.01 per cent of the total income of NR147,218 has been attributed to women. Total contributions have been calculated by aggregating the sectoral estimates.

(1983, Annex 1, table 6, p. 63)

Comments

"Although the statistical results obtained cannot be
generalised on the national level, the sample does represent a
fairly balanced cross section of Nepal's unusually diverse rural
population" (1981, p. 10).

(a)   "Concurrent activities performed by a single individual
were recorded separately, but our definition of double
activity was very strict: children playing with their
younger siblings did not count as 'child care'; child care
includes only feeding, carrying or direct attendance.

Intensity of work is a perpetually unanswered question
in all time allocation studies. In our study, all
activities are assumed to be of equal social value and
therefore we saw no need or practical means for
standardising the working hours by energy expenditure"
(1981, pp. 22-23).

"The fact that the aggregate data show women spending
almost as much time as men in salaried work is somewhat
misleading; salaried women are concentrated in only one
village and in the top stratum" (1981, p. 180).

(b)   "We did not set a monetary value for the services
produced within the household, i.e. services such as a
mother's care for her own children for which we do not feel
economic valuation is appropriate or feasible (1981, p.
14). We did not attempt to value those activities
traditionally defined as 'domestic' such as cooking,
laundry, cleaning and child care, partially because of the
difficulty in establishing a realistic wage for such
services in rural Nepal where there is ordinarily no market
for them. Another reason is that the value of many of
these services such as the preparation of a meal according
to strict rules of caste purity by someone who is vitally
concerned with the family's ritual status, cannot, in any
case, be adequately captured by purely economic measures"
(1983, p. 10).

Market prices. For goods available on the market,
prices at the nearest local market were used, averaged out
for seasonal variation if any (Status of Women Project
Team: Field manual ..., 1979, Appendix VI, Forms 70-72).
For goods not available on the market, the price of a
near-equivalent was used, according to the following
procedure. "To determine the value of dried vegetables
(which are hardly ever sold) such as gundruk, masuro, simki,
etc., we asked how many meals were produced for the whole
family. We then asked what the price would have been to
buy the cheapest vegetable, in the off-season, to feed the
whole family for one meal. We then multiplied the number
of meals of dried vegetables times the cost of one meal's
worth of the cheapest vegetables. Thus a conservative

replacement cost approach was adopted for valuation of these goods" (1981, p. 15 and Status of Women Project Team: <u>Field manual</u> ..., 1979, Appendix IV, p. 5).

(b) (c)   "Part of the reason for children's relatively low contribution to household income is that one of their major tasks is the undemanding - but also fairly unproductive - work of minding the family's animals" (1981, p. 177).

ALAUDDIN, 1980

Contribution of housewives to GNP: A case study of Pakistan

Purpose

"To evaluate the non-monetary work of housewives, ... to determine the factors that influence the time spent at home or the home production ..., and to incorporate them into a system of national accounts" (p. 5).

Method

Wage, substitute household worker, specialised and value added, at price of equivalent market product

(a) Micro-economic evaluation

The data come from a random sample of 259 urban households in the city of Lahore, during the period 1975-76. "The respondent is the 'housewife' defined as a woman who runs a home and takes care of domestic affairs provided that such a home includes one or more of the woman's immediate relatives" (p. 7).

Value of meal preparation, child care, house cleaning and laundry computed as:
time devoted to those activities (collected by recall for the day prior to the interview)
multiplied by
wage rates for those activities (p.10).

Value of knitting, sewing, food preservation, soap-making, basket weaving, spinning, etc. for the family (pp. 18 and 20) computed as:
volume of production (number of sweaters, etc.)
multiplied by
price of market equivalent
minus
input costs (monetary outlays for raw materials) (p.10).

(b) Macro-economic evaluation

     Value of housework, computed in (a)
        multiplied by
     total urban female population.

Results

(a)   In the sample, "on an average, a housewife spends about 9.5 hours per day on household activities. Cooking and meal preparation take up about 60 per cent of total time spent; house-cleaning, 19 per cent; child care, 20 per cent" (pp. 18-19). "Children aged 0-1 year take about two hours of attention and care daily, those aged 1-5 years about 1.4 hour, and those between 5-15 years, 1.2 hour. The average time spent on children aged 0 to 15 years is about 1.74 hour daily" (pp. 15 and 19).

    In the sample "on an average, a housewife produces goods and services worth Rs.448.79 per month, which increases the average household income from Rs.1,180.32 per month to Rs.1,629.00 per month, i.e. the value of housewives' production is about 38.03 per cent of household income" (p. 23).

    These values vary with household income; the two following tables show the value of housewives' production in relation to household income.

(b)   "If the value of housewives' production is included in the Gross National Product (GNP), the latter increases from Rs.121,298.00 million to Rs.163,170.07 million annually. That is to say, the value of their home production is about 35 per cent of the GNP. It is believed that this value of home production would be much greater if rural areas were included (where 80 per cent of the total population belongs), because a greater number of rural women are employed in activities of which no account is taken, and if the contribution of other family members were taken into account" (p. 30).

(a)

Value of housewives' production by household income groups

Monthly house-hold income (in Rs.)	Total no. of house-holds	Value of housewives' production and number of respondents in each group							
		0-50	50-100	100-150	150-300	300-500	500-800	800-1 200	1 200-2 000
100-500	39	-	-	7	8	24	-	-	-
500-800	68	-	1	2	26	37	2	-	-
800-1 200	65	-	-	2	22	33	5	3	-
1 200-2 000	58	1	2	4	10	25	6	5	5
2 000-3 000	23	-	-	-	1	8	6	4	4
3 000-4 000	5	-	-	-	-	1	1	2	1
4 000 +	1	-	-	-	-	-	-	-	-

(Appendix, table 4, p. 37)

(a)

Average value of housewives' production, per income bracket

Average house-hold income (in Rs.)	No. of house-holds	Average value of housewives' production	
		(in Rs.)[1]	(in % of household income)
300	39	315	105
650	68	328	50
1 000	65	379	38
1 600	58	514	32
2 500	23	771	31
3 500	5	930	27

[1] Total value of household production for all households in an income bracket, divided by number of households.

(Computed from Appendix, table 4, p. 37)

Comments

(a)   "The average age of the housewives in the sample is 38
years.   Had the respondents' average age been lower, more
younger children would have been reported in the sample"
(p. 16).   The relative time taken up by child care would
consequently have been different.
         These are very rough estimates.   They indicate that
the absolute value of household production increases with
monetary income but not as rapidly.   The relative economic
weight of household production in full income varies
inversely to income: household production doubles household
income in the lowest income bracket, while it adds only
about 30 per cent in the higher income brackets.

(b)   It is not clear from the publication why the total
number of urban females is used in the computation of the
macro-economic value of household production, instead of the
number of housewives.   Perhaps this procedure is used in
order to cover the entire population, rural and urban.   If
so - but no indications are given in the paper to support
this hypothesis - it would appear that only 20 per cent of
the urban females are housewives: the other 80 per cent
would be used to compensate for the 80 per cent of females
who live in rural areas.

KING, 1978

Time allocation and home production in rural Philippine households

---

Purpose

To value home production (child care, food production, and other housework) and thus full income (home production plus monetary income) using the general analytic framework of the "New Home Economics".

Method

Opportunity cost of time

The data come from a representative sample survey of 573 rural households in the province of Laguna, in April 1975. Time allocation data for father, mother and children collected by recall (past week for non-seasonal activities and over a longer period for seasonal activities).

The value of home production is given by:
time allocated to home production
    multiplied by
wage rates.

Results

"The time allocation data reveal that home production is of greater economic importance than market production in these households." No aggregate data are reported in this publication.

---

* See also Philippines 2-6 for other studies using the same data base.

The father contributes	57 per cent of market income, but only 34 per cent of full income.
The mother contributes	20 per cent of market income and 42 per cent of full income.
The children contribute	22 per cent of market income and 23 per cent of full income if school time is not valued; 32 per cent of full income if school time is valued (p. 201).

Comments

Evaluating home production time at the market rate "produces an underestimate of the value of home production because the average product of home-time should exceed the marginal product of home-time which in equilibrium should be equal to the wage rate" (pp. 200-1).

"The recall method used here understates the market production time for all children. The observation method [used in a subsample of 97 households at three intervals between September 1975 and March 1976] measured more than three times as much market production time for children" (p. 188).

CABAÑERO, 1978

The "shadow price" of children in Laguna households

___

Purpose

"To measure the costs ("shadow price": commodity outlays and time) and the contributions (both in home and market production) of a child to the household" (p. 63).

Method

The data come from a representative sample survey of 573 rural households in the province of Laguna from April 1975 to March 1976. Market wage data are derived from this sample while time-allocation data were collected by observation from a subsample of 99 households including 416 children.

Two types of wage rates are estimated: the market wage and the imputed "home" wage.

"The market wage refers to the average wage rates in all economic activities, weighted by the proportion of time spent in each activity" (pp. 77-78).

Returns in other activities

The "home" wage is computed by multiplying the gross output value of home-produced goods for household consumption and for sale (farm tools; furniture and fixtures; woodwork and woodcraft; repairs; home-sewn clothes; embroideries; woven materials; food preparation; washing clothes for others) by the share of the individual's time in total household time devoted to this production (p. 79). This "home" wage rate is utilised in valuing all home production including child care and housework.

___

* See also Philippines 1 and 3-6 for other studies using the same data base.

Results

In general, home wages are higher than market wages for all income classes, holding age constant.

Average hourly rates of child, by age group, income class and type of wage

Age group	Market wage			Home wage		
	Income classes			Income classes		
	Low	Middle	High	Low	Middle	High
3–5	0.66	0.74	0.70	1.06	1.24	1.27
6–8	0.66	0.46	0.97	0.93	1.29	1.13
9–11	0.66	0.57	1.00	0.94	1.19	1.35
12–14	0.84	0.92	0.95	1.08	1.17	1.13
15–17	0.90	1.03	1.27	0.95	1.10	1.27
18 and over	0.89	1.02	1.21	1.07	0.38	1.19

(Table 7, p. 80)

Comment

"This procedure assumes that all persons are equally productive" (Evenson, 1978, p. 28).

The comparison between "home wages" and market wages is interesting, particularly from the point of view of household resources (labour) allocation. Unfortunately, these home wages are calculated from gross output value in household production, not from value added which would be required for determining actual returns to labour in household production.

NAVERA, 1978

The allocation of household time associated with children in rural households in Laguna, Philippines

---

Purpose

Evaluation of economic contribution and of cost of children in order "to give some empirical content to the hypothesis that children in rural households do contribute positive economic time benefits to the household, and that it is a strong motivation for the household to have a relatively large number of children" (p. 204).

Method

Volume of labour inputs, in time

Data come from 99 rural households surveyed in the province of Laguna in September 1975 and March 1976. Time allocation data collected by observation of all household members: all family members, household help and relatives living under one roof and sharing the same food supply (p. 205).

The time costs of children include child care time (feeding, watching and bathing infants, etc.) and a share of other home production activities (dishwashing, clothes care, cooking and house cleaning). It is assumed that the time costs of home production activities are uniformly distributed among household members.

The time contributions of the child include activities for the market, for care of other household children and for home production activities (pp. 206 and 211).

---

* See also Philippines 1, 2 and 4-6 for other studies using the same data base.

Results

"The time cost per child is highest during the first two years of the child, averaging 5 hours per day; it thereafter decreases and levels off at 1.3 hours from age 12 and over.

The child begins to contribute economic time to the household as early as at age 3-5, though in negligible amounts. At age 10-11, he contributes about 2 hours per day, and his net time contribution already becomes positive.

The net time contribution reaches a peak of 5 hours per day at age 20 when the child's interests begin to move out of the household" (p. 211).

YBAÑEZ-GONZALO and EVENSON, 1978

The production and consumption of nutrients in Laguna households: An exploratory analysis

---

Purpose

Effort to investigate the demand for nutrients and the role of home production in the general analytic framework of the "New Home Economics", treating nutrients as the arguments of the utility function instead of foods (pp. 136 and 150).

Method

Opportunity cost of time and volume of output, by activity

The data come from a representative sample survey of 573 rural households in the province of Laguna, from April 1975 to March 1976. Data on actual dietary intake by individual household members, on food utilised, on food preparation and cooking time, and on home capital come from a subsample of 97 households.

"In equilibrium, the household produces for its own consumption, a bundle of nutrients such that the marginal utility per shadow price unit of each nutrient will be equal" (p. 147). "Demand functions for nutrients are specified in which the determinants of equilibrium levels of calories, proteins, vitamins A, etc. consumed are: (1) price of raw foods, (2) prices of household time inputs, and (3) 'fixed' or environmental factors influencing home production, such as homemaking skills and household capital" (pp. 136-7). Raw food is valued at constant market prices (p. 147). The educational and employment status of the mother are proxies for the value of her time

---

* See also Philippines 1-3 and 5-6 for other studies using the same data base.

(p. 142). The production function of nutrients by the household is estimated by regressing the volume of household output (aggregate nutrient intake) on the value of household inputs.

Results

"The cooking time variable appears to be highly significant and indicates a high marginal value of cooking time (about 2 pesos per hour at the geometric mean of the sample. [As a point of comparison, the mean food expenditure per capita per day is pesos 2.40 (table 1, p. 138).] We must acknowledge, however, that this variable may be reflecting other factors. Households with lower values of time also have low real incomes, ... may spend more time in food preparation and purchase more nutrients per peso expended" (p. 150).

"The marginally significant coefficient on the capital variable indicates a low realised rate of return on this investment (less than 2 per cent). The variable indicating whether the mother was employed in the market or not was not significant" (p. 150).

Comments

"The important fact that the economic value and importance of food preparation and cooking time have been shown to be determinants of nutrient intake does not provide a full test for treating nutrients as the direct object of utility. Such analysis would require data where food prices vary" (p. 15).

"It should be acknowledged that consumers do not necessarily derive utility primarily from nutrients. Qualitative aspects such as taste are surely important and they may be better captured by food units than by nutrients units" (p. 137).

EVENSON, POPKIN AND KING-QUIZON, 1980

Nutrition, work, and demographic behaviour in rural Philippine households

---

Purpose

"Attempt to measure full income in terms of payments to productive resources, which include, in addition to conventional market income, the value of time devoted to home production [(child care, food preparation and other housework)] plus the value contributed to home production by home capital" (p. 292). "We review some of the measurement objectives of the [Laguna] surveys and discuss the problems and limitation encountered. We do so in part to caution the reader about data quality" (p. 291).

Methods

The data are derived from: a representative sample survey of 576 rural households in Laguna province in 1975; a further intensive survey of a subsample of 99 households in 1975 and 1976; and a re-survey of 245 households of the 1975 sample and of 340 households of a 1963 sample in 1977 (pp. 64 and 289).

<u>(a)</u>   Volume of labour inputs, in time

Time use data were collected by recall in the initial 1975 survey and in the 1977 re-survey, from the wife (about home production) and from the husband (about market production). Time use data were collected by observation in the 1975-76 intensive survey (p. 297).

---

* See also Philippines 1-4 and 6 for other studies using the same data base.

(b)   Opportunity cost of time

    "The estimates of the value of home production are
obtained by using Gronau's methodology   (Gronau, 1976).
They are based on home-time allocation regression estimated
for employed fathers, mothers and children [1975-76
observation data]. These estimates are quite similar to
those computed simply by multiplying home time by wage
rates" (p. 336).

(c)   Wage, substitute household worker

    "We attempted to obtain 'alternative wages' for tasks
which family members perform but for which hired labour is
also sometimes employed" (p. 293).

Results

(a)   "Taking the amount of time spent on an activity as a
     measure of its importance, the data provide an indication of
     the magnitude of the under-measurement problem of household
     income" (p. 29?).
     The household members' contributions to total market time
and to home production time appear different depending on whether
data were collected by recall or by observation, as summarised in
the table below.

	Total market time %	Home production time %
1975 recall data		
Father	63	5
Mother	22	70
Children	15	25
1975 observation data		
Father	46	6
Mother	17	34
Children	37	60

    Child care requires 14.43 hours per week (recall data),
of which 10 hours (69 per cent) are provided by the mother
and 4 hours (26 per cent) by older children.

Asia, Philippines 5, cont.

(b)   "This calculation, while crude, indicates that home production is actually of approximately equal value with income conventionally measured" (p. 293).

The values shown in the table below are obtained on the basis of the 1975-76 intensive survey data.

	Value (pesos per year)	%	Excl. school time	Incl. school time
Market income				
Father	3 334	58		
Mother	1 148	20		
Children	1 301	22		
Total	5 783	100		
Home production				
Father	668		11	9
Mother	3 287		55	43
Children (excl. school time)	2 061		34	–
Total (excl. school time)	6 016		100	
Children (incl. school time)	3 599		–	48
Total (incl. school time)	7 554			100
Full Income				
Father	4 002		34	30
Mother	4 435		38	33
Children (excl. school time)	3 362		28	–
Total (excl. school time)	11 799		100	
Children (incl. school time)	4 900		–	37
Total (incl. school time)	13 337			100

(Derived from table 11.20, p. 335)

"Farming households have somewhat higher home production than non-farming households [Note: This result reflects the larger time inputs of farming households: 154.6 vs 147.8 hours per week (see table 11.3, p. 296)]. Home production is higher in households where the mother is not employed, and in households with a greater number of children [Note: Again a reflection of time inputs (tables 11.17 and 11.18, p. 331)]" (p. 336 and table 11.19).

(c) No values reported.

Comments

(a)   For the recall data, "we had problems with
double-counting of time such as in handicraft and home
gardening, the products of which may be partly sold and
partly consumed at home.   Such time was then reported by
the wife and the husband as both home and market
production; the portion of time spent in growing
home-consumed products was difficult to separate from the
portion spent in growing the marketed product.   We
arbitrarily classified as market activity any home time in
which all or part of the product was sold" (pp. 297-8).

For the observation data, joint activities are recorded
separately which entails double-counting of time (days total
more than 24 hours).

"Some observer bias was noted as the presence of the
observer appeared to influence activities, particularly on
the first days: a two-day approach was then used and the
first day's data was discarded" (p. 298).

"If we regard the observation data to be the more
accurate data, we have evidence that fathers tend to
overstate their market time and mothers tend to overstate
their home production time in recall.   Of more
significance, however, is the large understatement of both
market and home time of children in recall: parents tend to
view many home activities as leisure rather than production"
(pp. 298 and 301).   N.B. Recall and observation data
reported in this publication for home production are not
comparable, as the latter include school time while the
former do not.

(b)   The values of market income for the three categories of
household members reflect the wage differentials they
encounter in the market for their labour inputs.   For a
labour input representing 46 per cent of total household
time (a), the father generates 58 per cent of the
household's market income.   For labour inputs representing
respectively 17 and 37 per cent of total household market
time, the mother and children respectively generate 20 and
22 per cent of the household's market income.

KING and EVENSON, 1983

Time allocation and home production in Philippine
rural households

_____

Purpose

"To analyse the determinants of time allocation in rural
households by adapting the general body of modern household
economics theory to the low-income rural household setting.   To
use this analysis as the basis for a discussion of the value of
home production and of the need to include that value in any
estimates of full income of rural households" (p. 35).

Methods

(a)   Volume of labour inputs, in time

Time allocation data for father, mother and children
collected by recall (past week for non-seasonal activities
and over a longer period for seasonal activities) from 376
rural households, and by observation in a subset of 99
households, in the province of Laguna in 1975-76.   A
resurvey of 245 households was performed in 1977.

(b)   Opportunity cost of time

"Home production time-allocation regressions are used
to estimate the marginal product of home time;   they are
based on time allocation [and market wages] of _employed_
fathers, mothers and children from the 99 households
subsample in 1975.   It might also be noted that the

_____

* See also Philippines 1-5 for other studies using the same
data base.

estimates are quite close to those obtained simply by multiplying home time by wage rates" (pp. 49-50).

Results

(a)   "The average household allocates about 15 hours a day to market production and 12 hours a day to home production (excluding school time). Approximately 3 hours daily are spent on child care (including bottle-feeding, breast-feeding, and storytelling). Slightly more time is spent on food preparation, and about 6 hours are spent daily on other home production tasks (excluding school time)" (p. 38).
Of total market time:
the father contributes   46 per cent,
the mother contributes   17 per cent,
the children contribute 37 per cent.
Of home production time:
the father contributes   11 per cent,
the mother contributes   60 per cent,
the children contribute 29 per cent, excluding school time.

(Calculated from data on p. 38).

(b)   Values (table 3.8, p. 50) are the same as those reproduced in Philippines(5), Results, (b) (Evenson et. al, 1980).

Comment

(a)   The weekly "recall" and the daily "observation" methods for data collection on time use yield very different results, particularly in the 1975 survey. Although the recall questions were revised in the 1977 survey to improve accuracy, other problems subsisted which affected data compatibility (pp. 59-60). It is not clear from this publication, how all these problems were overcome, in order to achieve "average" household time allocation estimates.

EVERS and KORFF, 1982

Urban subsistence production in Bangkok

Purpose

To calculate the quantitative amount of subsistence production within a study of the social organisation of the reproduction of labour power in urban areas and particularly the combination of subsistence production and other uses of labour (pp. 4 and 24).

Method

Volume of labour inputs, in time

The data are derived from case studies observed in Klong Toey, a slum suburb of Bangkok. Time use data were collected for all household members. Subsistence production includes cooking, washing, housekeeping, construction of own house, etc. (pp. 3 and 24).

Results

For the urban households under consideration, 24 per cent of the total working time of all household members was used for subsistence production (p. 24).

Subsistence production in % of total working time	% of households
0	6
0.1 - 10	13
10.1 - 20	25
20.1 - 30	19
30.1 and more	37
	100

(Table, p. 24)

Comments

[In our Jakarta study (Evers, 1981a and b)], "shadow prices had to be used, especially for housework, though we were painfully aware that the use of market prices for use-value oriented subsistence labour was against the intrinsic logic of subsistence production. In our study in a Bangkok slum we used time budgets only" (Evers, 1984, p. 12).

"Whoever has time and the necessary competence engages in subsistence production. In other words, the labour power not used for earning money is used for subsistence production" (p. 20).

"Households regarded as very poor are small households which lack sufficient labour. In these households nearly all labour power has to be used for earning an income so that there is simply no more time left for subsistence production. Some services and goods provided through subsistence production in larger households have to be purchased by households with little available labour power" (p. 22).

"The possible reduction of subsistence production over time is not a result of 'modernisation' but a result of the destruction of the means of reproduction or of the access to them for people. Slum eviction has to be seen as a step into this direction. The people in the slums know that eviction and life in the flats reduces considerably their possibilities for subsistence production; for them, the slum is the place where reproduction under deteriorating circumstances is still possible. For the urban planner it is a mere cancer in the city" (pp. 29-30).

KRITZ et al. 1984

Argentina: El trabajo doméstico no remunerado en un época de crisis*

Purpose

To determine the importance of unpaid household work as a survival strategy in economic recession with, therefore, particular emphasis on low-income (poor) population strata (p. 22).

Method

Volume of labour inputs, in time

Time devoted by all household members to housework, care of children and health-care of adults. Given by a representative sample survey including 400 multi-person households, conducted in September-October 1983 in Gran Buenos Aires.

Results

These urban households devote an average of 84.5 hours per week to unpaid domestic work, i.e. 12 hours per day, Sundays and holidays included. Of this total, four-fifths or 69 hours per week, i.e. almost 10 hours per day, are performed by the housewife. The average domestic workload is 56 hours per week for employed housewives and 73 hours per week for non-employed housewives. The other household members each devote an average of 5.3 hours per week to domestic tasks (p. 25).

---

* Argentina: Unpaid domestic work in a period of economic recession.

Elements for a comparison with time inputs in the market sector:

"More than 1,300,000 workers in Gran Buenos Aires have working weeks of 45 or more hours. According to the definitions used by the National Institute of Statistics and Census, the normal work-week for paid workers oscillates between 35 and 45 hours (p. 24). Only 12 per cent of the housewives devote less than 40 hours per week to domestic tasks" (p. 27).

Comments

"Less than ten years ago, one minimum wage would almost meet the basic needs (i.e. the basket on which the consumer price index is calculated) of a family. In 1983, one out of three full-time workers (half of which work more than 45 hours) earns less than 35 per cent of the cost of such basket" (pp. 1-2). "Almost three out of four of the households surveyed have total monetary incomes of less than half the cost of the basket. The intensity of domestic activity observed is related to this recession: household tasks are more numerous and some become more time consuming (e.g., shopping more carefully and further away from home, making clothes and/or mending, etc.," (p. 31).

"Because of social attitudes, domestic tasks remain the women's role. The combination of the recession which increases women's market and non-market activities, and of a conservative division of household roles results in a large increase of women's workload and in a reduction of the time specifically devoted to child care" (p. 44).

TELLERIA GEIGER, 1983

Revalorización del trabajo doméstico*

Purpose

To try and determine the approximate value of domestic work at different social levels.

Methods

(a)   Volume of labour inputs, in time

Time devoted by all household members, including domestic servants, to housework and child care. Time allocation given by case studies conducted in eight La Paz households, interviewed and observed during seven days in October 1983.

(b)   Gross output value, at price of equivalent market product

Value of meals prepared at home, derived from price of meals in medium- and low-cost restaurants.

Results

(a)   For the eight households under consideration, the average daily time devoted, seven days per week, by household members and domestic servants to domestic activities is:

1 high-income household	(4 members)	15.5 hours
3 medium-income households	(5 members)	13.3 hours
4 low-income households	(4-9 members)	16 hours

---

*Revaluation of domestic work.

(b)   "In order to purchase all their meals in medium-price restaurants, the medium income households under consideration would have to spend monthly $b. 102,000" (p. 31).

"In order to purchase lunch and dinner in low-price restaurants, low income households would have to spend monthly $b. 54,000" (p. 36).

"As a point of comparison, the minimum legal wage was, at the same point in time, $b. 17,000" (p. 37).

Comment

"Case studies, with no pretence at statistical representativeness" (p. 2).

PARDO, 1983

La dueña de casa y su aporte al PGB* (I)

PARDO and CRUZ, 1983

La dueña de casa en sus actividades de trabajo: su valoración en el mercado y dentro del hogar** (II)

Purpose

To estimate the time housewives devote to domestic activities and to evaluate the product thus generated (I, p. 34) in order to complement the estimates of female activity levels yielded by Employment and Unemployment Surveys which exclude non-market work, and in order to determine the underestimation of the national product (II, p. 1).

Methods

(a)   Volume of labour inputs, in time

Time allocated to housework, child care and health care of adults by housewives, i.e. "by the persons responsible for domestic activities, whether they perform the work themselves or whether they supervise the work performed by others, and independently of whether they work in the market or not" (I, p. 34). Time allocation given by the Special Survey of Housewives conducted in July 1981 in Gran Santiago by the Department of Economics of the University of Chile on a representative sample (I, p. 35).

---

* The housewife and her contribution to the "gross geographical product" (GGP).

** The housewife and her work activities: their evaluation in the market and in the household.

Latin America, Chile, 1982, cont.

(b)   Wage, equivalent market function

Household work-time, as given in (a)
        multiplied by
"hourly wages paid in the market for performing activities equivalent to household activities" (I, p. 41), i.e., "paid in food industries, commercial laundries, child-care centres, etc." (I, p. 35).

(c)   Opportunity cost of time

Household work-time, as given in (a)
        multiplied by
"wages earned in the market by women (computed according to educational level, age and labour market experience from wage data given by June 1981 Survey of Employment and Unemployment in Gran Santiago, Department of Economics, University of Chile)".

Results

(a)   Housewives devote, in Gran Santiago, an average of 51.7 hours per week to domestic activities (37.9 hours for employed housewives; 56.3 hours for unemployed housewives). (For averages according to number and age of children, size of household, educational level of housewife, assistance by paid domestic worker or by unpaid family members, and income of household head, see I, p. 35.)

Gran Santiago housewives: imputed wages for domestic activities and product generated

All domestic activities	Cooking, cleaning	Laundry, ironing	Shopping	Child care	Care of adults
Imputed hourly wages (in pesos of May 1981)					
(b) 39.34	45.61	33.32	31.55	31.55	81.14
(c) 46.91	-	-	-	-	-
Product (in percentage of "gross geographical product")					
(b) 15.1	6.5	1.9	2.1	4.1	0.5
(c) 18.0	7.7	2.3	2.6	4.8	0.6

(Tables 5 and 7, pp. 40 and 43)

"If Chile housewives are assumed to perform two-thirds of all domestic activities (as verified in other countries), then the household product generated by all household members in the nation's households would amount to more than 30 per cent of the GGP" (I, p. 44).

Comments

"The results are representative for urban Gran Santiago in May 1981. They are thus representative for 4 million citizens residing in a large city and corresponding approximately to 40 per cent of the country's total population. The extrapolation to all the nation's households is much weaker" (Pardo, Private communication, June 1986).

"Differences in the wages used for the imputations explain the differences between the values obtained with the two [monetary] evaluation methods. It should be noted that the average opportunity cost wage [forgone wage] is higher than the imputed wages obtained through the other method, except for the activity 'health care of adults' which corresponds to a relatively high market wage" (II, p. 48).

"The housewife's decision to work in the labour market is essentially determined by the wage she can command in the market and by the household income level. As for the first, it can be observed that it takes relatively high wage levels for a housewife to quit household work in order to enter the labour force. As a result, one may suppose that a high value is attached to the work she performs in the household. This is particularly true at high levels of household income. At low income levels, participation in the labour force is the result of a survival need; labour force activity alternates with frequent withdrawals determined by fluctuations in the need for her household work" (II, pp. 50-51). Pressure for monetary income combined with household needs for essential domestic activities drives many women into assuming a double load of work: housewives in the labour force totalise, on the average, 86.8 hours of work per week (I, p. 39, note 6) for domestic and market oriented activities.

MARTINEZ ESPINOZA, 1983

El valor del trabajo doméstico de la dueña de casa*

Purpose

"To update information yielded by 1981 Special Survey of Housewives (see Pardo and Cruz, 1983), to analyse in more detail the characteristics of household work and the factors which determine it, and to estimate the contribution of household work to family welfare in Chile" (pp. i and 17).

Methods

(a)   Volume of labour inputs, in time

Time allocated by all household members older than 6 to housework, care of children, health care of adults, repair of dwelling, of appliances and of vehicles, care of animals and garden, etc. Time allocation given by case studies conducted in 24 families of Gran Santiago in July 1983 by the Institute for the Study of Labour Relations and Management (IDERTO) of the University of Chile (pp. i and 17).

(b)   Wage, substitute household worker and wage, equivalent market function

Household work-time, as given in (a)
     multiplied by
weighted imputed wages determined as follows.

A national inquiry was made about the hourly wages paid for market services similar to those provided by domestic activities (p. 23). These wages are those paid to female domestic servants (polyvalent), to specialised household workers (seamstresses of different skill levels), and to

---

* The value of the housewife's domestic work.

employees performing, in market enterprises (restaurants, hotels, commercial laundries, children's day-care centres, etc., p. 8) tasks similar to those performed in households (cook and cook aid, laundress, electrician, plumber, car washer, baby-sitter, employee in children's day-care centres, day nurse, night nurse, clerical employee, etc., Annex 3). These wages are grouped according to the corresponding domestic activity (food preparation; cleaning and repair of dwelling, laundering and ironing, etc.) For each category of activity, an average imputed wage is calculated, weighted according to estimates of the time the housewife devotes to various aspects of the activity and of the skills required.

(c)   Opportunity cost of time

Household work-time, as given in (a)
              multiplied by
imputed forgone wage "calculated on the basis of a regression equation adjusted on the wages earned by housewives working in the labour market" (p. 25).

Results

(a) Time allocation data tabulated for housewives only.
    For the 24 families under consideration, the average weekly time devoted by housewives to domestic activities is shown in the following table.

All housewives	Employed housewives		Unemployed housewives	
	With children younger than 6	Without children younger than 6	With children younger than 6	Without children younger than 6
(24)	(5)	(6)	(7)	(6)
Average time per week, in hours				
[61]	57	29	100	49

(Table 7, p. 19)

For the 24 families under consideration, the imputed hourly
wages of the housewife's time are:
(b)   food preparation: 91 (pesos, July 1983)
      cleaning and repair of dwelling, laundering and ironing: 104
      sewing: 101
      care of children: 108
      health care of adults: 64
      miscellaneous: 60
      [Reference market wages are: domestic servant: 65; cook:
      130; cook aid: 78; seamstress: 80 to 200; baby-sitter:
      200; day nurse: 63; clerical employee: 72.   (Annex 3)]
(c)   Employed housewives,
         with children younger than 6   : 175 (pesos, July 1983)
         without children younger
         than 6   : 105
      Unemployed housewives,
         with children younger
         than 6   : 162
         without children younger
         than 6   : 77
      Total, all 24 housewives   : [144]

(Table 10, p. 26)

For the 24 families under consideration, the average monthly
imputed value of housewives' domestic activities is shown in the
following table.

All housewives	Employed housewives		Unemployed housewives	
	With children younger than 6	Without children younger than 6	With children younger than 6	Without children younger than 6
(24)	(5)	(6)	(7)	(6)
Average monthly value, in pesos of July 1983				
(b) [24 000]	23 000	11 000	40 000	19 000
(c) [35 000]	58 000	11 000	54 000	16 000
As a percentage of household monetary income*				
(b) [33]	32	18	61	22
(c) [48]	80	19	82	18
* Household monetary income:				
[73 000]	73 000	62 000	66 000	87 000

(Table 11, p. 28)

Comments

"There is no claim as to the representativeness, on a national basis, of the sample under study. It is probable that national averages would come close to the lowest figures, as the majority (75 per cent) of housewives in Gran Santiago (and supposedly in the whole country) fall in the category 'without children younger than six' ... and because our sample includes women of higher educational level than the national average (83 per cent of the sample housewives had secondary or higher education, while the corresponding estimate for Gran Santiago is 42 per cent)" (p. 29).

<u>(a), (b), (c)</u> The overall averages (in brackets) are not meaningful on a national basis, as the 24 families do not constitute a representative sample. Differences between subset averages are to be interpreted with caution as they are based on data collected from four to six families.

<u>(b), (c)</u> These two evaluation methods differ: wages for categories of domestic activities <u>(b)</u> are computed on an entirely different basis from wages by occupational status <u>(c)</u>.

<u>(a)</u> Because of data collection methodology and evaluation methodology <u>(b)</u>, simultaneous tasks are counted separately. For instance, all child-care time (primary and secondary activity) is included; as a result, the time allocated by housewives to "care of children" ranges from seven to 94 hours per week (Annex 2, table c). This data is therefore not comparable with studies that only include primary activities. The convention used in this study requires that the corresponding time allocations not be confused with housewives' "hours on duty".

<u>(b)</u> "Wages of domestic servants may significantly underevaluate the work of a housewife because of differences in quality and efficiency. At the wages of employees working in [commercial] services, the value of a housewife's work is subject to distortions; overevaluation and underevaluation" (p. 8). "The value obtained with this method is particularly influenced by the presence of children less than six years old (large time inputs and high market wages)" (p. 23).

Because of double counting of time for simultaneous tasks (see comment <u>(a)</u>), this method perhaps yields an overestimate of the value of housewives' domestic work. For instance, for child care, a baby-sitter (at 200 pesos an hour) may give fuller and more active attention to a child than a mother "keeping an eye" on the child while performing household chores. (We are stressing that there might be an economic overevaluation; in no way are we claiming that fuller attention is better education-wise.)

Latin America, Chile, 1983, cont.

(c)   "Evaluation at opportunity cost of time likely tends to overevaluate domestic work" (p. 9).

Double counting of time for simultaneous tasks is definitely inadequate for this evaluation method. What would be relevant here is time on duty (see comment (a)). Double counting leads to an overestimate. Differences between the values obtained with (b) and (c) are therefore to be interpreted with caution.

RENDON, 1979

El ama de casa productera de millones* (Cited in: Pedrero, 1983, p. 34.)

Method

Wage, substitute household worker, polyvalent

Results

Household production by housewives in 1970 Mexico City amounted to a figure similar to the GDP generated in the agricultural sector.

---

* The home-maker producer of millions.

PEDRERO NIETO, 1983

El valor económico de las actividades domésticas; aproximaciones
metodológicas con información mexicana*

Purpose

To establish approximate estimates of the value of household
productive activities, and to discuss, through the Mexican
example, the methodological problems encountered and their
possible solutions.

Methods

(a) Volume of labour inputs, in workers

Critical analysis of 1970 Census data (persons, mostly
women, registered as "not in the labour force" by age and
matrimonial status; number of households; number of
dwellings; number of families) in order to determine the
number of persons who have major responsibilities in
domestic activities.

(b) Gross output value and Value added, derived from consumer expenditures

The gross output value of household-prepared meals is
calculated as follows:
consumer expenditures for food and beverages consumed in
households (National Survey of Households, Income and
Expenditures, 1977)
    multiplied by
a coefficient borrowed from market enterprises. (The
coefficient - 3 - is the multiplication factor restaurants

---

* The economic value of domestic activities; methodological
approximations based on Mexican data.

apply to the price of their raw materials in order to determine the price to be charged to customers; it covers all expenses including overheads, taxes and entrepreneurial margin.)

The expense forgone as a result of unpaid household work in food preparation (cooking and serving meals; dishwashing and cleaning up) is equated to:

gross output value of household-prepared meals

minus

expenditure for food and beverages consumed in households.

(c)   Opportunity cost of time

Unpaid household work performed by housewives is evaluated at the average wage earned by females of the same educational level in Mexico City (2nd trimester 1978).

(d)   Wage, substitute household worker, polyvalent

Unpaid household work performed by housewives is evaluated at the wage earned by domestic workers in Mexico City (1978).

Results

(a)   9.5 million persons devote themselves essentially to the daily reproduction of the labour force (p. 13). (No figure is given such as total population, or labour force, which would permit a comparison.)

(b)   "60 per cent of the population (the poorest first six deciles; those who spend more than 50 per cent of their income on food) would need more than twice their present monetary income if they were to pay for the food they now prepare for themselves" (p. 20).

As shown in the following table, for the lower six income deciles of the population, one single household activity (food preparation) produces an income in kind larger or equal to their monetary income. For the highest decile, this income in kind is equal to half the monetary income.

Expense forgone in food preparation

Household deciles	Total monetary expenditures (in thousand pesos)	Expenditures for food consumed at and away from home (% of total expenditure)	Forgone expense as a result of food preparation at home (% of total expenditures)
I	3 515 239	65.30	125.5
.	.	.	.
.	.	.	.
.	.	.	.
VI	22 523 141	56.44	105.2
.	.	.	.
.	.	.	.
.	.	.	.
X	105 493 814	30.75	50.6

(Excerpted from table 2, p. 25)

Housewives, in 1978, in Mexico City, produced an income in kind evaluated as follows:
(c) 7,363 million pesos i.e. 193 per cent of the monetary income earned by women in the labour force;
(d) 2,353 million pesos i.e. 62 per cent of the monetary income earned by women in the labour force.

Comments

"Because of lack of data, our figures constitute only rough evaluations; they should not be considered final evaluations" (p. 47).
(b)   The forgone expense (value added by household production) is estimated at twice the monetary cost of food consumed in the household production process. This rule of thumb is utilised in order to make up for missing statistical data, namely the actual market value of meals equivalent to those prepared in households.
"Our calculations are given as ... exercise, ... illustration. They could be refined by adjusting for taxes, by accounting for differences in quality for the use of semi-prepared food; the validity of coefficient '3' would have to be checked in the context of household production, etc." (pp. 18; 20-21).
"These calculations could be extended to the other services provided by household work, including child care,

bearing in mind that certain activities such as personal relations (expressions of affection, etc.) and biological reproduction - although they are very important for society and although they consume time and energy - would not and should not be accounted for in economic terms" (p. 21).

(d)   Wages of domestic servants are the lowest of all in 1978 in Mexico City.

TUEROS, HOYLE and KRITZ, 1984

El trabajo doméstico no remunerado en dos distritos de Lima*

Purpose

To determine time devoted to domestic activities by housewives and to analyse the impact of socio-economic circumstances.

Method

Volume of labour inputs, in time

Time allocated by housewives to housework, child care, health care of adults, care of garden and plants, etc. Time allocation given by 48 case studies conducted in two districts of Lima: Villa María del Triunfo (VMT), a poor neighbourhood (6.5 members per household; US$ 36 monthly per capita income; informal sector occupations) and Jesús María (JM), a middle-class neighbourhood (4.1 members per household; US$ 100 monthly per capita income; wage employment mostly as employees and liberal professions).

Results

The average weekly time, including Sundays and holidays, devoted by housewives to unpaid household activities is 64.5 hours in the 24 VMT households, and 59.5 hours in the 24 JM households.

---

* Unpaid domestic work in two districts of Lima.

Comments

"Time does not reflect the physical effort required for the performance of a task. For instance, when a woman declares she spends six hours on laundering in VMT, this is the time physically devoted to the task, while, in JM, this is usually the time during which the clothes washer is in operation. While the latter is work (not only mechanical, but also requiring a personal effort), the technical component is different and the physical requirement is one-fifth or one-sixth of the former. It is therefore important to take into consideration the intensity of household work. [In addition,] women in VMT spend more time on heavy tasks than in JM. For instance, they spend 33 per cent more time on laundering and ironing. ... The only exception in which middle class women work more on a heavy task than poor women is house cleaning [because of] larger dwellings, more elaborate furniture and higher social value placed on cleanliness" (pp. 11, 13-14).

"Food preparation requires 25 per cent more time in VMT, 24.5 hours weekly as compared to 19.5 in JM [because of] larger families, less satisfactory equipment (one out of five VMT housewives cooks on coal or wood fuelled stoves), more time required for food purchasing: 42 per cent of VMT housewives go to distant places for better bargains, using unsatisfactory public transportation. Their weekly shopping time is 6.5 hours against 4 hours for JM housewives who also buy food outside their neighbourhood (two out of three housewives) using their own private transport" (p. 16).

"Child care takes an average of 23.5 hours per week in VMT and 20 hours in JM. [Physical care] of children takes 50 per cent more time in VMT (18.5 hours weekly), while 'reading unrelated to schoolwork' absorbs an average of 17 minutes in VMT against 1.5 hours in JM. ... Supervision of school work takes the same amount of time in both neighbourhoods. In the context of unfavourable circumstances, VMT housewives concentrate their efforts on those tasks which are indispensable for the regular functioning of the household, and the supervision of schoolwork is part of this routine, while 'reading unrelated to schoolwork' appears as an extra which, in addition, requires an inclination deriving from a higher educational level of the parents" (pp. 18-19).

"A final comment ... JM housewives devote an average of 8.5 hours per day, including Sundays and holidays, to unpaid household work. Such a high figure in a neighbourhood as well off as JM leads us to raise the hypothesis that, in Peru's present recession, unpaid household work constitutes a mechanism for adjusting to the decrease of family income, not only among poor households, but also, in a rather similar way, among a large impoverished sector of the middle class" (pp. 19-20).

CAMPIOTTI, 1983

Valor económico de las actividades del hogar: Uruguay*

Purpose

"Attempt at outlining a methodology for the determination of the economic and social value of household work, by using as indicator the time required for the performance of household tasks ... to experiment a method, and to propose operational and theoretical hypotheses to be checked through further studies" (pp. I and II).

Method

Volume of labour inputs, in time

Time allocated by all household members older than 6 and by non-household members giving unpaid assistance with household activities, to housework, child care and physical care of adults, repair of dwelling, of furniture and of vehicles, heating, care of animals and garden, etc. Time allocation given by case studies conducted in 35 Montevideo households in September 1983.

"It appears feasible to determine, among household activities, the average number of work hours required for an adult, an adolescent, a child, an infant or a handicapped person. In this manner, it would be possible to reach estimates to be incorporated in national accounts studies" (p. 57).

---

* Economic value of household activities: Uruguay.

Results

For the 35 households under consideration, the <u>average weekly time</u> devoted by household members and non-household members to unpaid household activities is given in the following table.

Household type[1] (number)	Housewife only	Housewife and other women	Husband and other males	All household and non-household members
		(hours per week)		
A (7)	64	74	38.5	112.5
B (10)	48	61	36.5	97.5
C (11)	55	61	5.5	66.5
D (5)	26	33	8.5	41.5
E (2)	49	49	–	49
		(percentage of total time)		
A (7)	57	70.5	29.5	100
B (10)	49.1	70.5	29.5	100
C (11)	82.6	92.5	7.5	100
D (5)	61.6	84.4	15.6	100
E (2)	100	100	–	100

[1] A: urban marginal or informal sector; low income; low educational level. B: modern sector; low income; low educational level. C: modern sector; average income; average educational level. D: modern sector: higher income; secondary and higher education. E: modern sector; highest income levels; secondary and higher education (p. 24). For finer specification, see appendix of original publication.

(Derived from pp. 39-40)

"Food preparation, provisioning and laundering, i.e. personal survival activities, are the predominant activities in informal sector, low income, low education households" (p. 31). When moving up the socio-economic ladder, a higher proportion of time is devoted to house cleaning, supervision of children, school work, etc., with food preparation remaining a dominant activity. Food preparation consumes 39 per cent of the total unpaid household work time of the 35 families under consideration. "50 per cent of unpaid household work is performed in the kitchen" (p. 27).

"The time devoted weekly to unpaid household work in the 35 families under consideration is 20 hours per person in the household. This figure is not representative statistically, but it allows an interesting approximation: taking into account the average household composition (3.274 members in Montevideo) and the percentage of economically active (38.7 per cent), we can deduct that households devote an average of 65 hours per week to unpaid household work, and an average of 61 hours per week in the urban modern sector (assuming that all the economically active work in this sector), i.e. households devote an equal number of hours to unpaid household work [and to market-oriented activities]" (p. 25).

Comments

"These values cannot be generalised on a statistical basis ... not only because they are derived from case studies, but also because the cases were purposedly selected for illustrating typologies ... which take into account demographic, cultural, social stratification and environmental variables bearing on household activity and on its economic evaluation" (pp. 24, 55 and 13).

Note: This study offers an interesting graphical presentation (circular, on a logarithmic scale) of the distribution of unpaid household work time among different groups of activities.

VALECILLOS et al. 1983

División del trabajo, distribución personal del tiempo diario y valor económico del trabajo realizado en los hogares Venezolanos*

Purpose

To determine the prevailing pattern of time-allocation among the adult population, and to estimate the economic value that should be imputed to the unpaid household work of housewives.

Methods

Volume of labour inputs, in time

(A) Time devoted by housewives i.e. "married women and women heads of households" (p. 90) to housework and child care. Estimated, on the basis of conservative assumptions, from official labour force data (Venezuela, Oficina Central de Estadística e Informática, 1982). Housework time of employed housewives is estimated to be 66 hours (i.e. an hypothetical maximum of time devoted weekly to productive activities) minus labour force time. Housework time of non-employed housewives is estimated to lie between 20 and 45 hours per week, depending on age, i.e. in relation to household size and responsibilities. Includes urban and rural areas.

(B) Time allocation by all adult household members, i.e. males and females over 18 years of age. Given by an ad hoc representative sample survey conducted, in July 1982, in the ten largest cities and totalising approximately 1,000 households and 2,650 adults.

---

* Division of labour, personal distribution of daily time, and economic value of the work performed in Venezuela's households.

(a)   Opportunity cost of time and
                    wage, average for female workers

Household work time (A and B)
     multiplied by
average wages in their occupation for employed housewives
and average wages of all female workers for non-employed
housewives.

(b)   Wage, substitute household worker
                 and wage, average for female
                 workers in service occupations

Household work time (A and B)
     multiplied by
average wages of domestic servants and of women in service
occupations ("the two categories of average wages being, by
coincidence, very similar") (p. 161).

(c)   Wage, equivalent market function

Household work time (B)
     multiplied by
average wages in market enterprises (restaurants, commercial
laundries, child-care institutions, etc.) performing
functions similar to household activities.

Results

(A)   Housewives devote an average of 34.1 hours per week to
     domestic activities.
(B)   In urban areas, adult males devote an average of 6.5
     hours per day (Sundays and holidays included) to productive
     activities, out of which 0.5 hour (8 per cent) is for unpaid
     household work. Adult females devote 7 hours per day to
     productive activities, of which 4.75 hours (68 per cent) are
     for unpaid household work.
          Housewives' household production, if included in the
     national income, would have increased it by an amount which
     varies depending on the time estimate used (A or B) and on
     the wage (a, b or c) used for the evaluation. The results
     of the corresponding combinations (Aa, Ab, Ba, Bb and Bc)
     are given below:
     (Aa) 37 per cent   (Ab) 20 per cent   ---
     (Ba) 41 per cent   (Bb) 22 per cent   (Bc) 34 per cent

                                             (pp. 160-175)

Comments

Hours of time in (A) and (B) are derived from different sources, and (B) covers only urban areas. However, the aggregate numbers of hours for housewives differ only by 5 per cent (p. 167). (A) gives a somewhat higher estimate for employed housewives and (B) for non-employed housewives.

"20 to 22 per cent are minimal evaluations related to the fact that female wages in the domestic and service occupations are the lowest of all" (p. 162).

"37 to 41 per cent are not maximal evaluations as they still reflect that women's wages are 59 per cent lower than men's" (p. 159). [This paper also presents evaluations based on men's wages; they are discussed in section 4.4 of the present monograph.]

"20 per cent, the lowest evaluations, are very close to the value of the product of the petroleum sector, and are much larger than any other single economic sector" (p. 20).

Oceania
KIRIBATI and TUVALU
(formerly Gilbert and Ellice Islands)
1972-74
urban and rural

GILBERT ISLANDS, 1979

National accounts 1972-74

Purpose

   "The national accounts should cover not only those goods and
services which are exchanged for money, but must also attempt to
value the important range of goods used by people in their daily
living which they produce for themselves" (p. 3).

Method

Minimum wage

   "Also included in the category of industries are the
own-account activities of households; use and construction of
dwellings, non-residential buildings and other projects by
households; own-account production of commodities by households,
where the activities have not already been set off as industries
by virtue of the fact that the households sell the products on
the market" (pp. 81-82).
   "The principles followed are those recommended by Dommen
(1974) slightly amended, extended along the lines of the Papua
New Guinea National Accounts" (p. 88 and private communication,
April 1979).
   Time-use data for the rural areas come from a
government-sponsored Rural Socio-Economic Survey in five
islands.   "In urban areas, it has only been possible to make
estimates of a few of the non-monetary activities carried out"
(pp. 88-89).
   Among the activities "considered to be economic in nature"
(p. 89), the following are relevant for the present study:
handicrafts, thatching, breadmaking, carting water, house and
other capital repairs.
   "The hours of work have been adjusted by an 'activity'
coefficient to allow for [variations] in energy and

concentration, from task to task, between areas and between children and adults.

The adjusted mean labour inputs per household per year are
    multiplied by
the estimated number of households (1968-73 Census extrapolation)
    and by
the average wages of unskilled rural labour.

Where there were identifiable cash inputs (e.g. in breadmaking, cash inputs are assumed to be equivalent to three-quarters of gross value) and cash sales (e.g. for handicrafts, as recorded in the monetary accounts), the value of these was deducted" (pp. 89, 90 and 93).

Results

Non-monetary production by activity (A$'000s)

	1972	1973	1974
1. Work on land			
.			
.			
.			
8. Handicrafts	209	266	305
9. Thatching	41	42	46
10. Breadmaking	3	3	4
11. Carting water	35	37	40
12. Services of owner-occupied dwellings)[1]	207	211	237
Total, non-monetary production	1 830	1 939	2 279
Per capita, total	32	33	39
Total, monetary production	13 982	20 286	34 220
Total, gross domestic product (at current purchasers' values)	15 812	22 226	36 499

[1] "House and other capital repairs" (p. 89).

(Excerpted from table 1, p. 35 and table 6, p. 94)

Comments

"The extent of exchange of goods and services for cash in rural areas, for those products typically produced in a non-monetary context, is limited in the Gilbert and Ellice Islands, and although this type of exchange appears to be becoming more common, sales of e.g. babi and toddy tend to be conducted at arbitrarily agreed rates of exchange that cannot be said to approximate 'market' prices. There is only one organised market for local foodstuffs in the territory, which has a relatively low turnover" (p. 88). Labour inputs have therefore been used as the basis of the evaluation instead of physical output at market prices.

"The carting of water was included as it absorbed a significant proportion of household time and can be considered as analogous to water distribution by tanker in urban areas. Food preparation was excluded as being analogous to household preparation of purchased food, by convention excluded from national accounts, although for some commodities (e.g. te tuae) the processing could be classified as manufacturing" (p. 89).

"Activity coefficients have been deduced from a number of sources and from discussions with a number of individuals. [Although these coefficients] are of necessity somewhat arbitrary, a surprising degree of unanimity as to appropriate values was achieved" (pp. 89 and 91).

"Data were not available in sufficient detail to isolate skilled tasks (e.g. canoe building) and all labour inputs were thus classified as unskilled. Labour has been valued at the average rate paid by local government councils, as this information was readily available and is a good approximation of other rural wage rates" (p. 90).

"In the South Pacific Region a relatively large proportion of the output of households is not marketed, although it is doubtful whether there remain any households that are not at least to a minor degree involved in the cash economy. In the Gilbert and Ellice Islands the highest proportion of non-monetary income as estimated here was, in one area, slightly more than 60 per cent of total estimated household disposable income. There appear at the other extreme, however, to be very few households in which there is no non-monetary activity, even in areas of widespread cash employment" (p. 88).

Given that "activity coefficients" were applied to hours of work, given that minimum wages were used, and given that cash inputs were deducted (in our opinion, an inappropriate procedure when the evaluation is based not on gross output value but on time inputs), the evaluation of non-monetary production arrived at is probably an underestimate.

Oceania
PAPUA NEW GUINEA
1960-74
urban and rural

PAPUA NEW GUINEA, Bureau of Statistics, 1974

National accounts statistics 1960-61/1973-74

Purpose

"One of the principal objectives of the United Nations System of National Accounts (SNA), on which the Papua New Guinea system is modelled, is to measure the total value of goods and services produced in an economy ... For purposes of comparison between countries and from one period to another, it is important that national accounts should cover not only the production of goods and services which are sold (exchanged for money) but also the production of similar goods and services for use by the producer on own account. This is particularly true in respect of Papua New Guinea, where a considerable amount of production is not exchanged" (pp. 5 and 195).

"The rural village subsector of the households sector is in rapid transition as an increasing proportion of villagers supplement their production for own consumption with production for the market ... It is intended to develop [within] the national accounts system, a set of economic accounts for the rural village subsector which will assist persons concerned with rural development both in their planning and in monitoring the changes taking place in the subsector" (pp. 195-196).

Methods

"Several types of imputations have been made in compiling the national accounts in order to cover own-account activities of households, the contribution of free and partially paid labour provided in rural areas to various authorities, etc." (p. 14).

Among own-account activities of households, those relevant for the present study are: collection of firewood; construction and maintenance of dwellings, non-residential buildings and other projects; construction of equipment (canoes, cooking utensils and furniture) (pp. 7, 15, 35 and 200).

In the Papua New Guinea national accounts, the term "non-market" production applies only to own-account production occurring in traditional "rural villages". Own-account production occurring in urban and rural non-village areas is included in the market components of the accounts (p. 15).

(a)   Gross output, at price of equivalent market product

Firewood

Number of families in rural villages gathering firewood (estimated)
    multiplied by
average quantity of firewood consumed per family per year (observed by field staff)
    multiplied by
average price of firewood in rural areas (observed by field staff) (p. 200).

No allowance is made for compensation of employees or consumption of fixed capital (p. 196). "It has not been possible to estimate the value of any transactions in the nature of intermediate consumption which may occur in the production process" (p. 15).

(b)   Minimum wage

Dwellings: equipment

Number of days per year spent on construction and repair
    multiplied by
minimum daily wage rate in rural areas (pp. 201-202).

Results

Detailed figures for selected activities are not given in the publication.

Comments

"It has not been possible to take into account, in the estimation procedure, any transactions (e.g. barter) between rural villagers which may occur in the production process: direct estimates have been made of the amount of own-account production for final use by all rural villagers as a whole" (p. 15).

Oceania, Papua New Guinea, cont.

"Valuation of production which is not exchanged for money is difficult; it can only be done by making somewhat artificial assumptions about the value to the producer/consumer of this output. In view of the relative importance of this production, such valuation has been made in preparing the estimates in this publication, but it should be recognised that even minor variations in the value assumptions would result in substantially different estimates for many of the aggregates shown, including gross domestic product, national income and national disposable income" (p. 188).

BIBLIOGRAPHY

The publications listed below are relevant to the subject of this study and were consulted in the course of its preparation. In Part I, no attempt is made at documenting every statement: quotations and references are kept to a minimum.

Aas, Dagfinn. 1982. Measuring the use of time, Special Studies, No. 7. Paris, OECD, Social Indicator Development Programme.

Abdullah, Tahrunnessa A.; Zeidenstein, Sondra A. 1982. Village women of Bangladesh: Prospects for change. Oxford, Pergamon Press, 246 pp.

Acharya, Meena; Bennett, Lynn. 1981. The rural women of Nepal: An aggregate analysis and summary of eight village studies. The Status of Women in Nepal, Vol. II, Part 9, Kathmandu. Tribhuvan University, Centre for Economic Development and Administration, 432 pp.

---; ---. 1983. Women and the subsistence sector: Economic participation and household decision-making in Nepal, Staff Working Paper No. 526. Washington, DC, The World Bank, Jan., 140 pp.

Ahmed, Iftikhar (ed.). 1985. Technology and rural women: Conceptual and empirical issues. London, Allen and Unwin.

Alauddin, Talat. 1980. Contribution of housewives to GNP: A case study of Pakistan. M.S. thesis, Vanderbilt University, Nashville, Tennessee, 46 pp.

Anker, Richard. 1978. Demographic change and the role of women: A research programme in developing countries. Geneva, ILO, Nov.; mimeographed World Employment Programme research working paper; restricted.

---. 1983a. Effect on reported levels of female labour force participation in developing countries of questionnaire design, sex of interviewer and sex proxy status of respondent: Description of a methodological field experiment. Geneva, ILO, July; mimeographed World Employment Programme research working paper; restricted, 82 pp.

---. 1983b. "Female labour force participation in developing countries: A critique of current definitions and data collection methods", in International Labour Review (Geneva), Vol. 122, No. 6, Nov.-Dec., pp. 709-723.

---; Buvinić, Mayra; Youssef, Nadia H. (eds.). 1982. Women's roles and population trends in the Third World. London, Croom Helm, 287 pp.

---; Hein, Cathryn (eds.). 1986. Vers la mesure des activités économiques des femmes. Geneva, ILO.

---; ---. (eds.). Medición de las actividades económicas de la mujer. Geneva and Santiago, ILO, forthcoming.

Archambault, Edith. 1984a. "Travail domestique et emploi tertiaire: Substitution ou complémentarité", in Vernières (ed.), 1984, pp. 189-205.

---; Greffe, Xavier (eds.). 1984b. Les économies non officielles. Paris, Editions La Découverte, 248 pp.

Barkay, Richard, M. 1982. "National accounting with limited data; Lessons from Nepal", in Review of Income and Wealth (New Haven, Connecticut), Series 28, No. 3, Sep., pp. 305-323.

Becker, Gary, S. 1965. "A theory of the allocation of time", in Economic Journal (Cambridge), Vol. 75, No. 299, Sep., pp. 493-517.

Benería, Lourdes (ed.). 1982. Women and development: The sexual division of labour in rural societies. New York, Praeger, 261 pp.

Bério, Ann-Jacqueline. 1983. Time allocation survey: A common tool for anthropologists, economists, and nutritionists. Paper presented at the Symposium on Food Policy, XIth International Congress of the International Union of Anthropological and Ethnological Sciences, Vancouver, 20-25 August, 36 pp.

---. 1984. The use of time allocation data in developing countries, from influencing development policies to estimating energy requirements. Paper presented at International Research Group on Time Budgets and Social Activities Meeting, Helsinki, August, 33 pp.

Binswanger, Hans, P.; Evenson, Robert, E.; Florencio, Cecilia, A.; White, Benjamin, N.F. (eds.). 1980. Rural household studies in Asia. Singapore, Singapore University Press, 369 pp.

Birdsall, Nancy. 1980. "Measuring time use and non-market exchange", in McGreevey (ed.), 1980, pp. 157-173.

Blades, Derek W. 1975. Non monetary (subsistence) activities in the national accounts of developing countries. Paris, OECD, 99 pp.

---. 1982a. "The hidden economy", in OECD Economic Outlook: Occasional Studies (Paris), June, pp. 28-45.

---. 1982b. "The hidden economy and national accounts", in OECD Observer (Paris), No. 114, Jan., pp. 15-17.

Botswana, Ministry of Finance and Development Planning, Central Statistics Office, 1976. The rural income distribution survey in Botswana, 1974-75. Gaborone, Government Printer, 291 pp.

Boulouiz, Bouchra. 1983. Travail féminin et espace domestique: Approche dans le cadre d'un espace sous-développé; le cas du Maroc. Thèse pour le Doctorat de troisième cycle, UER de Sciences Economiques, Université de Paris X, Nanterre, 241 pp.

Buvinić, Mayra; Lycette, Margaret, A; McGreevey, William Paul. 1983. Women and poverty in the Third World. Baltimore and London, Johns Hopkins University Press, 326 pp.

Cabañero, Teresa A. 1978. "The 'shadow price' of children in Laguna households", in Philippine Economic Journal (Quezon City), Vol. 17, No. 1-2, pp. 62-87.

Cain, Mead T. 1977 and 1980. "The economic activities of children in a village in Bangladesh", in Population and Development Review (New York), Vol. 3, No. 3, Sep. 1977, pp. 201-228. Also published in Binswanger et al. (eds.), 1980, pp. 218-247.

---; Khanam, Syeda Rokeya; Nahar, Shamsun. 1979. "Class, patriarchy and women's work in Bangladesh", in Population and Development Review (New York), Vol. 5, No. 3, Sep., pp. 405-438.

Cairncross, Sandy; Cliff, J. Forthcoming. "Water use and health in Mueda, Mozambique", in Transactions of the Royal Society of Tropical Medicine and Hygiene (London).

Campiótti T., Juan L. 1983. Valor económico de las actividades del hogar: Uruguay. Montevideo, Apr., 68 pp. Mimeographed. (Excerpts included in ILO, Regional Office for Latin America and the Caribbean, 1984.)

Carr, Marilyn. 1985. "Technologies for rural women: Impact and dissemination", in Ahmed (ed.), 1985, pp. 115-153.

Chayanov, A.V.. 1966. The theory of peasant economy. Homewood, Illinois, American Economic Association.

Dahl, Hans Erik. 1979. Rural production in Botswana 1974-75: A national accounts analysis of the Rural Incomes Distribution Survey. Economic Papers, No. 17. Bergen, University of Bergen, June, 376 pp.

De Serpa, A.C. 1971. "A theory of the economics of time", in Economic Journal (London), Vol. 81, No. 324, Dec., pp. 828-846.

Dommen, Edouard C. (ed.). 1974. Estimating non-monetary economic activities: A manual for national accounts statisticians, Paper prepared by a working group on "The subsistence sector in the South Pacific" convened by the University of the South Pacific, 12-22 August. Suva, Oct.

Elwert, Georg; Wong, Diana. 1980. "Subsistence production and commodity production in the Third World", in Review (Binghamton, New York), Vol. 3, No. 3, winter, pp. 501-522.

Erasmus, Charles J. 1955. "Work patterns in a Mayo village", in American Anthropologist (Washington, DC), Vol. 57, No. 2, Part 1, Apr., pp. 322-333.

Evenson, Robert E.; Popkin, Barry M.; King-Quizon, Elizabeth. 1980. "Nutrition, work and demographic behaviour in rural Philippine households: A synopsis of several Laguna household studies", in Binswanger et al. (eds.), 1980, pp. 289-366.

Evers, Hans-Dieter. 1981a. "The contribution of urban subsistence production to incomes in Jakarta", in Bulletin of Indonesian Economic Studies (Canberra), Vol. XVII, No. 2, July, pp. 89-96.

---. 1981b. Subsistence production and wage labour in Jakarta. Working Paper No. 8. Bielefeld (Federal Republic of Germany), University of Bielefeld, Sociology of Development Research Centre, 30 pp. Mimeographed.

---. 1984. Wage labour, subsistence production and basic needs. Unpublished paper presented at informal ILO/WEP seminar, 25 Sep.

---. Korff, Rüdiger. 1982. Urban subsistence production in Bangkok. Working Paper No. 25. Bielefeld, University of Bielefeld, Sociology of Development Research Centre, 36 pp. Mimeographed.

---; Pitomo, Sundoyo; Betke, Friedhelm; Buckholt, Helmut. 1982. A survey of low income households in Jakarta: Selected summary tables. Working Paper No. 17. Bielefeld, University of Bielefeld, Sociology of Development Research Centre, 72 pp. Mimeographed.

Fawcett, James T. (ed.). 1972. The satisfactions and costs of children: Theories, concepts, methods. Summary report and proceedings of the workshop organised by the East-West Population Institute, Honolulu, 27-29 April. Honolulu, East West Center.

Feachem, Richard G.A.; Burns, Elizabeth; Cairncross, Sandy; Cronin, Aron; Cross, Piers; Curtis, Donald; Khalid Khan M.; Lamb, Douglas; Southall, Hilary. 1978. Water, health and development: An interdisciplinary evaluation. London, Tri-med Books, 270 pp.

Fisk, E.K. 1975a. "The response of non-monetary production units to contact with the exchange economy", in Reynolds (ed.), 1975, pp. 53-83.

---. 1975b. "The subsistence component in national income accounts", in Developing Economies (Tokyo), Vol. XIII, No. 3, Sep., pp. 252-279.

Folbre, Nancy. 1984. "Household production in the Philippines: A non-neoclassical approach", in Economic Development and Cultural Change (Chicago), Vol. 32, No. 2, Jan., pp. 303-330.

Gaertner, Wulf; Wenig, Alois (eds.). 1984. The economics of the shadow economy. Springer Verlag, Berlin.

Gilbert Islands, 1979. National accounts 1972-74. Bairiki, Tarawa Government Printing Division, Apr., 95 pp.

Glaude, Michel; Moutardier, Mireille. 1982. "L'évolution des niveaux de vie de 1966 à 1979", in Economie et Statistique (Paris), No. 142, Mar., pp. 21-40.

Goldschmidt-Clermont, Luisella. 1982. Unpaid work in the household: A review of economic evaluation methods, Women, Work and Development 1. Geneva, ILO, 148 pp.

---. 1983a. "Does housework pay? A product-related microeconomic approach", in Signs (Chicago), Vol. 9, No. 1, autumn, pp. 108-119.

---. 1983b. "Output-related evaluations of unpaid household work: A challenge for time use studies", in Home Economics Research Journal (Washington, DC), Vol. 12, No. 2, Dec., pp. 127-132.

---. 1986. "Le travail non-rémunéré au foyer: Synthèse critique des méthodes d'évaluation économique", in Anker and Hein (eds.), 1986, pp. 39-87.

---. Forthcoming. "Trabajo no remunerado en el hogar; un análisis de los métodos de evaluación económica", in Anker and Hein (eds.), forthcoming, Ch. III.

Gronau, Reuben. 1976. Who is the family's main breadwinner? The wife's contribution to full income. Paper No. 148. Stanford, California, National Bureau of Economic Research, Sep.

Guyer, Jane I. 1978. "The food economy and French colonial rule in Central Cameroon", in Journal of African History (Cambridge), Vol. 29, No. 4.

Hart, Gillian. 1980. "Pattern of household labour allocation in a Javanese village", in Binswanger et al. (eds.), 1980, pp. 188-217.

Harvey, Andrew S. 1979. "The role of time-budgets in national and regional economic accounting", in Michelson (ed.), 1979, pp. 11-22.

---; Macdonald, W. Stephen. 1976. "Time diaries and time data for extension of economic accounts", in Social Indicators Research (Dordrecht), Vol. 3, No. 1, June, pp. 21-35.

Hawrylyshyn, Oli. 1977. "Towards a definition of non-market activities", in Review of Income and Wealth (New Haven, Connecticut), Vol. 23, No. 1, Mar., pp. 79-96.

Henn, Jeanne Koopman. 1978. Peasants, workers and capital: The political economy of labor and incomes in Cameroon. Cambridge, Massachusetts, Harvard University, 405 pp. Ph.D. dissertation.

Ho, Teresa Jayme. 1979. "Time costs of child rearing in the rural Philippines", in Population and Development Review (New York), Vol. 5, No. 4, Dec., pp. 643-662.

ILO, Bureau of Statistics. Forthcoming. Surveys of economically active populations: A manual on concepts and methods. Geneva.

---, Regional Office for Latin America and the Caribbean. 1984. Mujeres en sus casas: Estudio sobre el trabajo no remunerado en el hogar. Excerpts of papers presented at: Taller informal de consulta sobre el valor económico de las actividades del hogar, Lima, 24-27 Apr., 145 pp.

---, Thirteenth International Conference of Labour Statisticians (Geneva, 18-29 Oct. 1982). 1983. Resolution I: "Resolution concerning statistics of the economically active population, employment, unemployment and underemployment."

India, Central Statistical Organisation (CSO). 1981. National accounts statistics. New Delhi.

International Association for Research in Income and Wealth and United Nations, Economic Commission for Africa. 1983. Actes de la Conférence régionale africaine, Douala, 15-20 Nov. 1982. Paris, Institut National de la Statistique et des Etudes économiques et Ministère des Relations extérieures, Coopération et Développement. 2 vols., 680 pp.

Jain, Devaki; Banerjee, Nirmala (eds.). 1986. Tyranny of the household. Delhi, Shakti Books/Vikas.

Johnson, R.W.M. 1961. On the valuation of subsistence production. Occasional Paper No. 1. Salisbury, University of the Rhodesias and Nyasaland.

King, Elizabeth. 1978. "Time allocation and home production in rural Philippine households", in Philippine Economic Journal (Quezon City), Vol. 17, Nos. 1-2, pp. 185-202.

---; Evenson, Robert E. 1983. "Time allocation and home production in Philippine rural households", in Buvinić et al. (eds.), 1983, pp. 35-61.

Kritz, Ernesto H. 1983. Trabajando en el hogar: Hacia una revalorización económica de las actividades domésticas. Lima, ILO, June, 40 pp. Mimeographed.

---; Acebo, Alberto; Cerri, Mario; Espinosa, Adriana; Garassino, Maria, A.; Welti, Ana, E. 1984. Argentina: El trabajo doméstico no remunerado en un época de crisis. Jan., 58 pp. Mimeographed. (Excerpts included in ILO, Regional Office for Latin America and the Caribbean, 1984.)

Komba, John M. 1983. "The subsistence sector in Tanzania", in International Association for Research in Income and Wealth and United Nations, 1983, pp. 113-124.

Kusnic, Michael W.; Da Vanzo, Julie. 1980. Income inequality and the definition of income: The case of Malaysia. Santa Monica, California, Rand Corporation (R-2416-AID). June, 121 pp.

Lancaster, Kelvin J. 1966. "A new approach to consumer theory", in Journal of Policital Economy (Chicago), No. 74, Apr., pp. 132-157.

Longhurst, Richard. 1982. "Resource allocation and the sexual division of labor: A case study of a Moslem Hausa village in Northern Nigeria", in Benería (ed.), 1982, pp. 95-117.

Lorfing, I.; Khalaf, M. 1985. The economic contribution of women and its effect on the dynamics of the family in two Lebanese villages. Geneva, ILO, May; mimeographed World Employment Programme research working paper; restricted, 38 pp.

Lucas, Robert E.B. 1981. Distribution of wages and employment in rural Botswana. Working Paper No. 43. Boston, Mass., Boston University, African Studies Center.

McGreevey, William Paul (ed.). 1980. Third-World poverty: New strategies for measuring development progress. Lexington, Massachusetts, and Toronto, DC, Heath and Company, 219 pp.

Macpherson, George; Jackson, Dudley. 1975. "Village technology for rural development: Agricultural innovation in Tanzania", in International Labour Review (Geneva), Feb., pp. 97-118.

Martínez Espinoza, Eduardo. 1983. El valor del trabajo doméstico de la dueña de casa. Santiago, Universidad de Chile, Instituto de Estudio de Relaciones del Trabajo y Organización. Oct., 46 pp. Mimeographed. (Excerpts included in ILO, Regional Office for Latin America and the Caribbean, 1984.)

Mehran, Farhad. Forthcoming. "The concept and boundary of economic activity for the measurement of the economically active population". Draft chapter; to appear in ILO, Bureau of Statistics, Manual on surveys of economically active populations.

Michelson, William (ed.). 1979. Public policy in temporal perspective. The Hague, Paris, New York, Mouton Publishers.

Mignot-Lefèbvre, Yvonne. 1978. "Les enjeux de la production domestique non-marchande en Afrique", in Revue Tiers-Monde (Paris), Vol. 19, No. 76, Oct.-Dec., pp. 819-830.

Minge-Klevana, Wanda. 1980. "Does labour time decrease with industrialization? A survey of time allocation studies", in Current Anthropology (Chicago), Vol. 21, No. 3, June.

Mueller, Eva. 1984. "The value and allocation of time in rural Botswana", in Journal of Development Economics (Amsterdam), Vol. 15, Nos. 1-3, pp. 329-360.

Mukherjee, Moni. 1983. Contributions to and use of social product by women. Paper presented at Workshop on Women and Poverty, Calcutta, Centre for Studies in Social Sciences, 17-18 Mar. 1983, 16 pp. Also published in Jain and Banerjee (eds.), 1986.

---. 1986. "Bread and roses", in Journal of Income and Wealth (Delhi), Vol. 8, No. 2.

Murray, Colin. 1976. Keeping house in Lesotho. Ph.D. thesis. Cambridge (United Kingdom), University of Cambridge.

---. 1981. Families divided: The impact of migrant labour in Lesotho. Cambridge, Cambridge University Press, 235 pp.

Nag, Moni. 1972. "Economic value of children in agricultural societies: Evaluation of existing knowledge and an anthropological approach for studying it", in Fawcett (ed.), 1972, pp. 58-98.

---; White, Benjamin N.F.; Peet, R. Creighton. 1978 and 1980. "An anthropological approach to the study of the economic value of children in Java and Nepal", in Current Anthropology (Chicago), Vol. 19, No. 2, June 1978, pp. 293-306. Also published in Binswanger et al. (eds.), 1980, pp. 248-288.

Navera, Emeline Realubit. 1978. "The allocation of household time associated with children in rural households in Laguna, Philippines", in Philippine Economic Journal (Quezon City), Vol. 17, No. 1/2, pp. 203-223.

Nectoux, François. 1979. Comptabilité nationale et structure sociale de la production en Afrique. Thèse pour le Doctorat de troisième cycle, Université de Paris I. 2 vols. 443 pp.

Neubauer, Herbert. 1985. "Schwarzarbeit und eigenleistungen in der österreichischen Bauwirtschaft", in Skolka (ed.), 1985a, pp. 131-160.

Oppong, Christine. 1982. "Family structure and women's reproductive and productive roles: some conceptual and methodological issues", in Anker, Buvinic and Youssef (eds.), 1982, pp. 133-150.

---; Abu, Katharine. 1985. A handbook for data collection and analysis on seven roles and statuses of women. Geneva, ILO, 134 pp.

Papua New Guinea, Bureau of Statistics. 1974. National accounts statistics: Principal economic accounts and supporting tables, 1960/61-1973/74, by R.W. Fergie. Port Moresby. Nov., 221 pp.

Pardo V., Lucía. 1983. "La dueña de casa y su aporte al PGB", in Revista de Economia (Santiago), No. 15, Aug., pp. 34-45.

---; Cruz N., Pablo. 1983. La dueña de casa en sus actividades de trabajo: Su valoración en el mercado y dentro del hogar. Documento Serie Investigación, No. 59. Santiago, Universidad de Chile, Departamento de Economia, July, 58 pp. Mimeographed.

Pedrero Nieto, Mercedes. 1983. El valor económico de las actividades domésticas: Aproximaciones metodológicas con información mexicana. Oct, 49 pp. Mimeographed. (Excerpts included in ILO, Regional Office for Latin America and the Caribbean, 1984).

Prest, A.R.; Stewart, I.G. 1953. The national income of Nigeria 1950-51. Colonial Research Studies, No. 11. London, HMSO, 123 pp.

Presvelou, Clio; Spijkers-Zwart, Saskia (eds.). 1980. The household, women and agricultural development. Wageningen, Veenman and Zonen, 130 pp.

Qah, Euston. 1985. "Household production and the measurement of economic welfare", in Indian Journal of Economics (Allahabad), Vol. 66, Part II, No. 261, Oct., pp. 243-258.

---. 1986. "Persistent problems in measuring household production: Definition, quantifying joint activities and valuation issues are solvable", in American Journal of Economics and Sociology (Lancaster, Pennsylvania), Vol. 45, No. 2, Apr., pp. 235-245.

Reid, Margaret. 1934. Economics of household production. New York, Wiley and Sons.

Rendón, Teresa. 1979. "El ama de casa productora de millones", in Fem (Mexico), cited in Pedrero Nieto, 1983.

Reynolds, Lloyd G. (ed.). 1975. Agriculture in development theory. New Haven and London, Yale University Press.

Rodgers, Gerry; Standing, Guy (eds.). 1981. Child work, poverty and underdevelopment. Geneva, ILO, 310 pp.

Schildkrout, Enid. 1981. "The employment of children in Kano, Nigeria", in Rodgers and Standing (eds.), 1981, pp. 81-112.

SEDES. 1966. Le niveau de vie des populations de la zone cacaoière du Centre-Sud Cameroun. Paris, Secrétariat d'Etat aux Affaires Etrangères, Chargé de la Coopération.

Simmons, E.B. 1975. "The small-scale rural food processing industry in Northern Nigeria", in Food Research Institute Studies (Stanford), Vol. 45, No. 2, pp. 147-161.

Skolka, Jiri V. 1976a. "Long-term effects of unbalanced labour productivity growth: On the way to a self-service society", in Solari and du Pasquier (eds.), 1976, pp. 279-301.

---. 1976b. "The substitution of self-service activities for marketed services", in Review of Income and Wealth (New Haven, Connecticut), Series 22, No. 4, Dec., pp. 297-304.

---. 1984. "The parallel economy in Austria", in Gaertner and Wenig (eds.), 1984, pp. 60-75.

---. (ed.). 1985a. Die andere Wirtschaft: Schwarzarbeit und Do-it-yourself in Oesterreich. Vienna, Signum Verlag.

---. 1985b. "Wende in der Arbeitsteilung", in Wirtschaft und Gesellschaft (Vienna), No. 4, pp. 445-469.

Solari, L.; du Pasquier, J.-N. (eds.). 1976. Private and enlarged consumption: Essays in methodology and empirical analysis. Amsterdam, North Holland Publishing Co.

Status of Women Project Team. 1979. Field manual: Guide-lines for the collection and analysis of data on the status of women in rural Nepalese communities. Kathmandu, Tribhuvan University, Centre for Economic Development and Administration. Dec., 120 pp. Mimeographed.

Szalai, Alexander (ed.). 1972. The use of time: Daily activities of urban and suburban populations in twelve countries. The Hague and Paris, Mouton.

Tellería Geiger, Gloria. 1983. Revalorización del trabajo doméstico. La Paz, Ministerio de Trabajo y Desarrollo Laboral, Instituto Nacional de Investigaciones Sociolaborales. (With the collaboration of Martha Urdininea). Apr., 45 pp. Mimeographed. (Excerpts included in ILO, Regional Office for Latin America and the Caribbean, 1984.)

Tomoda, Shizue. 1985. "Measuring female labour activities in Asian developing countries: A time allocation approach", in International Labour Review (Geneva), Vol. 124, No. 6, Nov.-Dec., pp. 661-676.

Tonga. 1980. National accounts estimates of the Kingdom of Tonga, 1974/75-1978/79. Appendix C: Methods of estimation and sources of data. Tonga, UNTCD Project, TON/78/001.

Tueros, Mario; Hoyle, Jenny; Kritz, Ernesto H. 1984. El trabajo doméstico no remunerado en dos distritos de Lima: Un estudio de caso en 47 familias de Villa María del Triunfo y Jesús María. Lima, Centro de Estudios para el Desarrollo y la Participación. Apr., 22 pp. Mimeographed. (Excerpts included in ILO, Regional Office for Latin America and the Caribbean, 1984.)

Turvey, Ralph. 1972. "The price of time in a technological age", in Quest (Dorking, United Kingdom), No. 22, autumn, pp. 30-37.

United Nations. 1986. The Nairobi forward-looking strategies for the advancement of women. As adopted by the World Conference to Review and Appraise the Achievements of the United Nations Decade for Women: Equality, Development and Peace, Nairobi, Kenya, 15-26 July 1985. New York.

---, Department of International Economic and Social Affairs, Population Division. 1982. Demographic indicators of countries: Estimates and projections as assessed in 1980. New York.

---, Economic and Social Council. 1984. Progress report on the review of the System of National Accounts (SNA): Report of the Secretary-General, Statistical Commission, Twenty-third Session, 25 Feb.-6 Mar. 1985. New York, 31 Oct. (E/CN.3/1985/5).

---, Statistical Office. 1968. A system of national accounts (Studies in Methods, Series F, No. 2, rev. 3). New York.

Valecillos T., Hector; U. de Ferrán, Lourdes; Ghavoum, Houda; Soto B., Carola; Gatrif, Ferez; Galindez, Edgar; Montero, Luis; Quidel, Patrick. 1983. División del trabajo, distribución personal del tiempo diario y valor económico del trabajo realizado en los hogares Venezolanos. Caracas, Banco Central de Venezuela. Nov. 289 pp. Mimeographed. (Excerpts included in ILO, Regional Office for Latin America and the Caribbean, 1984.)

Venezuela, Oficina Central de Estadística e Informática, 1982. Survey of households: First Semester. Caracas.

Vernières, Michel (ed.). 1984. L'emploi du tertiaire. Paris, Economica. 219 pp.

Ward, Michael. 1971. "Aspects of the official national income tables of Fiji", in <u>Review of Income and Wealth</u> (New Haven, Connecticut), Series 17, No. 3, Sep.

White, A.U. 1972. <u>Drawers of water: Domestic water use in East Africa</u>. Chicago, Chicago University Press.

Ybañez-Gonzalo, Susan; Evenson, Robert E. 1978. "The production and consumption of nutrients in Laguna households: An exploratory analysis", in <u>Philippine Economic Journal</u> (Quezon City), Vol. 17, Nos. 1-2, pp. 136-153.

Zeidenstein, Sondra A. (ed.). 1979. "Learning about rural women", in <u>Studies in Family Planning</u> (New York), Vol. 10, No. 11/12, Nov./Dec.